Behind Closed Doors

Book Two
The *Gypsy Moon* trilogy

By Veronika Sophia Robinson

Published by Starflower Press

Behind Closed Doors
Book Two, The *Gypsy Moon* Trilogy
© Veronika Sophia Robinson
© Cover illustration by Sara Simon
Author photograph by Dave Hollins

ISBN: 978-0-9931586-3-6
Published by Starflower Press
www.starflowerpress.com
June 2016
New Moon in Gemini: *The Storyteller's Moon*
British Library Cataloguing in Publication Data.
A catalogue record for this book is available from
the British Library.

Other novels by the same author:
Mosaic
Bluey's Café
Sisters of the Silver Moon

For the full list of the author's non-fiction titles,
visit: www.veronikarobinson.com

Dedicated, with love, to my family.
You are my whole world.

Behind Closed Doors

Summer

Wake Up!

Jolted from a dream—or was it a nightmare?—Azaria Linden woke with a start. Her moan brought Isaac's arm securely around her waist.

"Are you okay, sweetheart?" he asked tenderly, stroking her long, lustrous silver hair.

"Give me a minute," she pleaded, aligning herself somewhere between Dreamtime and morning. Azaria knew the dream was important, she could feel it in the shaking of her hands, and despite being fully awake now, she absolutely had to get back to it.

"You're crying," Isaac whispered.

Instinctively, Azaria's hand went to the corner of her eye.

"Yes," she replied softly, "but they're not *my* tears."

The gentle lullaby of sweet birdsong usually woke Azaria from slumber, but not today. Instead, the shock of her dream matched the drama of the fierce rain whipping against the window pane, and finally, the irate clap of thunder so ear-splitting it was as if the Great Hypnotist yelled "Wake Up!"

The white-feather and silver-bead dreamcatcher, handed down through four generations of women, mocked her as it hung in the window. *Damn you*, Azaria thought. And then the dream came back to her, clear as day. Azaria relayed it to Isaac: "Astrid wants to find her daughter. She's not said anything to me, but that dream…Oh, Isaac, it was so powerful. I feel like a truck has run over me."

He kissed her softly upon her cheek, and then suggested: "Maybe you should talk to her."

"*Me?* You know as well as anyone that Astrid and I

aren't close. Sure, we've been getting on just fine — really well, in fact — and I love her, I truly do, but we're light years apart on so many issues. Can you imagine if I said to her 'by the way, sis, I had a dream you wanted to find your daughter'?"

"It can't hurt, though."

"It *would*. It would hurt, and undermine the relationship I'm trying to build with her."

A mild knocking on the bedroom door ended their conversation.

"Gran?" Ruby's voice, soft and yearning, came from the hallway. "May I come in?"

"Of course you can."

Ruby's morning visits to their bed were becoming habitual. Not that Azaria minded. Nor Isaac. It was sweet that the teenager felt no self-consciousness about asking for comfort and companionship.

She snuggled in-between them, her long flaxen hair spread across the pillows, then said "I just had the strangest dream. I can't get it out of my head. Astrid was crying and asking Bob to help her find Victoria."

Azaria and Isaac looked at each other, surprised by the synchronicity.

"There's only one thing for it," Isaac said. He knew Azaria didn't want a bar of it. "You have to speak to Astrid. You don't have to tell her about the dreams, just broach the subject."

"Oh, I only had *one* dream," Ruby said, correcting him.

"I had the same dream," Azaria confessed.

"You did?" Ruby asked, her eyes growing full like the Moon.

"We were just talking about it before you came in."

"What are we going to do?" Ruby asked.

Azaria snuggled in closer to her granddaughter.

That Ruby was prepared to take responsibility for creating a major life change in this family filled Azaria with pride. Despite Ruby's slim body, she was one of the strongest females Azaria knew.

"I need some time to think about it," Azaria said. "You know what? I'm going up to the labyrinth." She thought of the last time she'd walked it, following Luna's death, and how grief-stricken she'd been. Until now, she hadn't been ready to face the pain again. Today was different. She needed answers.

"Why don't you and Isaac get some breakfast ready?" Azaria said to Ruby.

"Okay, Gran."

The heat of the shower was in stark contract to the cool tears which had awoken her. She dressed simply, in cotton shorts and a t-shirt, then Azaria strolled to the meadow, intent on finding an answer to her question. The journey to the meadow reminded her of rebuilding her relationship with Astrid. One path came instinctively, and the other was a struggle, but both were journeys mirroring her inner self. She hadn't been inside the labyrinth since the day her community came to help create it as a memorial to her late daughter, Luna. Today, she knew that it was finally time. Time to go within; time to seek an answer.

The rain had eased now. Wet and warm under her bare feet, the tender grass fashioned a soothing pathway up the field. The air, so muggy on this already claustrophobic Summer's morning, closed in around her as if ensuring she didn't go too far.

Standing on the outer circumference of the labyrinth, Azaria breathed in the lavender-scented air. This place was everything she dreamed it would be when the idea first came to her. She had felt the calling to expressed through structure. Something visible and tangible after her devastating loss. Her vision was that by moving through the labyrinth, the walker would leave behind their troubled thoughts, and reach a deeper level of awareness. Like life, it was about walking into the dark, to the stillness — perhaps to touch the face of the Goddess — and then back out into the world. Unlike a maze, Azaria knew there were no false turns: it was simply a matter of walking, one step at a time. There would be no getting lost.

She entered the mouth of the lavender labyrinth with grace, centring herself and connecting with the deeper purpose of the walk: *should she speak to Astrid about finding her daughter?*

Mindfully, taking one step at a time, the heady scent of lavender in full bloom cloaked her in calm, penetrating deep down into the layers of doubt. Time slowed down, and, as if in a different world, she soon emerged at the centre of the labyrinth. Azaria sat on the hand-carved wooden bench beside the sculpture of Luna. Her breath caught in her throat, the resemblance too much to bear. The life-sized bust of Luna's head and upper torso lying down in perfect stillness, as if asleep, on a bed of grass and wildflowers, shocked Azaria by how real it appeared. Made from a combination of coloured and clear glass in such exquisite detail, Azaria was surprised by the tears now falling, just as they had done on the day Luna's fiancé, Patrick, brought it to the farm

She gathered herself, then asked out loud: "So, Luna, what do you think? Should I talk to Astrid about finding Victoria? Even if she says yes, how on Earth would we find her? I don't have any answers..."

The leaden clouds of the early-morning thunderstorm were long gone, leaving behind a stifling sunny day. Azaria felt a distinct shift in the air, the storm had left a message that she couldn't ignore: *do something!* Upon her return to the farmhouse kitchen, Azaria found Isaac and Ruby laughing at the cat's antics.

Ruby looked up. "Hey Gran, watch this!" The short-haired Persian cat pawed at its reflection in the little mirror Ruby had placed in front of it.

"Shall we have breakfast on the veranda? It's far too warm to be stuck inside," Isaac suggested. "Ruby, you take the bowls. I'll bring the fruit salad."

"I'll fetch the tea," Azaria said, lifting the tray Isaac had already set out. "Is Car awake?"

"I'm right here." Car entered the kitchen, with a basket of laundry resting on her hip, and her long silver dreadlocks swaying as she walked.

Isaac whistled a tune as he left the kitchen, Ruby humming along. Azaria filled her mother in about the dreams.

"What do you make of it, Ma?" Azaria asked. "Ruby and I dreaming the same thing on the same night?"

Car's face lit up with joy at the possibility of Astrid looking for her daughter. "You've both had those dreams for a reason. Give it a day or two to settle within you, before you approach her."

"I think you're right." Azaria kissed her mother good morning, then said "Come on, let's eat."

They were about halfway through breakfast when Bob came striding over from the barn. Without Astrid. Azaria's heart sank. Since Astrid's cancer diagnosis, she and Bob went everywhere together. *Please, God, no,* Azaria prayed, hoping beyond hope her twin was still alive. They'd been estranged for most of their lives. Azaria wasn't ready for them to part when they were finally getting to know each other.

"Are you okay, Bob? You look really rough," Isaac

9

said, rising from his chair as Bob reached the veranda.

"I didn't sleep well," Bob said, running his fingers over his beard. "I haven't slept well all week." His eyes, the colour of a baby-blue sky, were bloodshot at the edges.

"Is it the mattress? Do you need a new one?" Azaria asked, concerned for their well-being, and riddled with guilt that she should be doing more to support them.

"No, the bed's fine." He paused, then pulled up a chair at the table, smiling at Azaria. "Everything about the loft is wonderful. We love living in there." He saw the concern on all their faces, and continued. "It's…It's just that Astrid keeps crying in her sleep. And all week she's…" He couldn't continue. The tears, liberated now that he had supportive company around him, fell freely. His voice cracked as he tried to find the words he so desperately wanted to share.

"It's okay, Bob, take your time," Isaac said kindly. He placed his hand on Bob's shoulder to reassure him.

"She calls Victoria's name in her sleep, like she's looking for her. But when she wakes up in the morning, it's as if nothing has happened. I don't know if she remembers her dreams or not, but it's disturbing me. I feel like I should say something, but we all know that's a wound she doesn't want to be uncovered."

"None of us can heal if we don't feel our pain fully," Car said kindly. "What's Astrid doing now?"

"She's sleeping. She exhausts herself at night, and has no idea why."

"Azaria?" Isaac said, prompting her to share the dream. He could see that she was reluctant to say anything that might lead to tension in her relationship with Astrid.

Ruby beat her to it. "Uncle Bob — Gran and I both had a dream that Astrid was asking you to find Victoria.

10

Both of us. On the same night! Can you imagine that?" Ruby's face lit up at the synchronicity. The freckles on her nose were more noticeable now that it was Summer.

"Really?" he asked, as if someone gave him permission to follow his gut instinct.

"Yes, it's true," said Azaria. "I woke up crying, but I knew they were Astrid's tears, not mine." Azaria poured herself another cup of orange-zest and ginger tea.

Bob stood up, and shook his head from side to side. He ran from the veranda back to the loft, his feet moving fast for a man who had recently celebrated his sixtieth birthday.

"I need to talk to you, Astrid" Bob said gently, as he woke her from another fitful dream. "You've been crying in your sleep all week. I don't know if you remember your dreams, but I can't go on like this. I don't want any secrets between us. I don't want you holding on to something and feeling like you can't share it with me. Astrid, I love you. You must know that nothing you can do or say will change that."

She nodded, then looked out the window, her eyes deliberately tracing the movement of the clouds. She thought about how fleeting the life of a cloud was, and how susceptible they were to air currents.

Similar in facial structure to Azaria, with high cheekbones and a beaming smile, Astrid's face was weary from cancer medication. Life had worn her down. She observed how easily the clouds could change direction.

"Bob, I want to find my daughter. I need to find Victoria," Astrid begged her husband, tears trickling down her cheeks. "I can't die without meeting her. It's important to me that I get to hold her. That I can look in her eyes and say how sorry I am. I've been too scared to ask before now. I feel so ashamed that I gave my own baby away. Victoria was so beautiful. I see her face so clearly even though it was forty-two years ago. I don't know how I could have just let her go. Will you help me find her?"

"I never thought you'd ask." If there was anyone who knew what would heal Astrid, it was Bob. For almost a year, he had barely strayed from her side as she fought valiantly against the disease which had riddled her frail body. Even before her diagnosis, he'd proved to be a faithful and devoted lover. Bob had felt the pain of her loss, but doubted that her stubborn pride would ever let her ask for his help.

Until Bob, Astrid had never known the healing power of love. Her previous experiences had all been traumatic. Bob's abiding love healed her in many ways, finally allowing her to see that she could reach out and find her long-lost daughter: the child she gave away at one day old. And, that, no matter what, he'd be there every step of the way supporting her.

"I don't know if it's even possible. It was a closed adoption," Astrid cried. Her face, screwed up with torment and guilt, reddened at the thought of the task ahead. "I was adamant that I never wanted to see her again."

"We'll find her. I promise we'll find her." Bob said, his hands massaging her rigid shoulders. He looked around the barn loft—decorated simply, but beautifully, with lush plants and woven rugs—grateful that they were here near her family. He knew he couldn't do this job alone. Finding Victoria would require everyone's support.

Astrid and Bob had been living in the loft of Azaria's apothecary barn, high on the Colorado mountain-top land, for more than six months now. The days had, to everyone's surprise, turned to weeks, and for some miraculous reason, months. Azaria's insistence that they live here nearby the family made perfect sense. It was too big a job for Bob to be a full-time sole carer. Azaria had her own selfish reasons, too, of course. She wanted to heal the relationship with her sister. Before it was too late.

Astrid talked Bob through the only day she'd ever spent with Victoria. Blinded by the grief of losing her husband in a fire, when she was just 16 years old, and just days before giving birth—a month before she was due—Astrid refused to keep their baby. Trauma closed her heart, like an immoveable vice, making the decades ahead a bitter and lonely road. But now, all these years later, the time had come to make another choice. She wondered if she had the strength to go through with it, and knew that her daughter had every right to refuse contact. As she contemplated the likely rejection she'd feel if Victoria declined a meeting, it hit Astrid hard in the gut to finally understand what it must be like for an adopted child to be given away by its parents.

She sobbed the morning away, stopping only to sip on sweetened hibiscus tea that Bob fetched for her at regular intervals. The only certainty in her life was that he was at her side. Always there. Always loving her. Eventually, tears gave way to slumber; there, on the sofa, she slept fitfully. Bob tucked a woollen blanket around her, smoothing his hand over her bald head. He was taken by surprise to see new hair growing at the back of her scalp. He flicked the pesky tears off his bearded jaw. He needed this. He needed hope. The past year had been so tough. The reality of the promise that he'd just made—to find Victoria—suddenly weighed heavy against his heart. Would he be able to find her? And, more importantly, would she be willing to meet Astrid?

Starr the Storyteller

Starr Linden reluctantly opened up her laptop. She tucked the edges of her chin-length bob of chocolate-coloured hair behind her ears, and got ready to write. Several months ago, she lost her beloved twin sister Luna in an earthquake in Honduras. Grief pummelled her on a daily basis, but writing was her salvation. Regular sessions with a grief counsellor barely helped her trudge the terrain of torment. But writing, oh writing was a balm! The days soldiered on, dragging her grudgingly forward into the future: a place without her sister. It was painfully hard being far away from her mother and family in Colorado, but she'd made a home here in Kununurra, in the far north of Western Australia, and separation was the price she paid.

She'd stepped into her journalist job at the newspaper with passion and determination, never imagining that shortly after arriving in Australia, her whole world would be blown apart. This temporary sabbatical, to work on a series of syndicated articles, gave her just the push she needed to start living again: to find her voice and sense of self now that her twin was no longer alive. She'd promised Luna, that day by the river, to live life for both of them. And that was what she was doing.

She drafted an outline for the editor: *Behind Closed Doors will feature several people and what happens in their lives that we don't see.*

A Skype alert flashed onto her screen. It was Uncle Bob. She clicked the icon, a smooth 's' against a sky-blue background.

"Bob? Hi! This is a surprise. Is aunty Astrid okay?"

Each day, Starr expected to hear the news that Astrid's journey through cancer was finally over. That she was at peace. Today wasn't that day.

"Don't worry, love. She's fine. She's still with us, fighting every day. Actually, she's the reason I'm skyping. I'm wondering if you might be able to help us."

"What do you mean?" she asked, raking her slender fingers through her hair. She still wasn't used to it being so short.

"It's time to find Victoria." He kept his voice low so that Astrid wouldn't hear his conversation. He needed to get things in motion without Astrid's knowledge. For now, at least. The last thing he wanted was to give his wife false hope.

Starr gasped. An unguarded cry, like the hesitant mewl of a newborn infant, escaped her mouth. The thought of Victoria, her cousin, finally being part of their family, seemed too much to take in.

"Really? Astrid wants to do that? *Now?* After all these years?"

She breathed out a long, slow, deliberate sigh of relief. "Oh my god, that's huge, Bob. Huge."

"Yes, love, it is. So will you help us?"

"Track her down? I can try."

One of Starr's key journalistic skills was that of investigation, but to find her cousin seemed way out of her skill set. There was just too little information to go on.

"Of course, Bob. Of course I'll do it. You'll need to refresh my mind about the details." Starr tilted her head back to make the most of the ceiling fan's cool air. "All I know is the hospital, date of birth, and parents' names. Is there anything else you can tell me?"

"Sweetheart, that's why I'm drafting you in! I have the names of a couple of midwives who were on shift that day, but that's as far as I've got. It was a closed adoption."

"Astrid gave up all her rights, didn't she?" Starr felt an anxiousness within at how Astrid must be feeling, and how hopeless the situation seemed. Starr knew the truth: finding her cousin was a long shot. "I can't promise anything. This is a tough one, on many levels, but what I can promise you is that I will leave no stone unturned. I'm about to take a couple of months off work from the newspaper so I can focus on the syndicated feature I'm doing. I'll fly home for a bit to look into this. Do me a favour? Don't tell Ma? I'd love to surprise her!"

"Sounds like just the tonic Azaria needs," Bob said gently, but his thoughts were focused on his wife.

"How's Mom doing?" Starr asked, a gulp, like a thudding grenade, strangling her Adam's apple.

"Isaac never leaves her side. If it wasn't for him and Car, I'm not sure. She's determined, and in fairness she's being kind to herself and not rushing the grief. You know what she's like: she keeps busy; but the hole Luna left behind isn't something that's going to go away. Ever."

"No it's not," Starr whispered, the loss a daily gulf in her heart, a wound so excruciatingly deep, she felt like razors had taken permanent residence in her belly. Holding back the tears, she said "I'll be in touch, Bob. Bye."

She exited Skype as quickly as she could, and fell onto her bed, overwhelmed, yet again, by the struggle of living without Luna. Would this pain never end? Why was it so hard to put one foot in front of the other? Not just today, but every damn day.

An hour later, she made herself a strong coffee. She could search for Victoria. She'd do it for Luna, and Azaria, Car, and Astrid and Bob: she'd bring her cousin home. Back to the family where she belonged. A family that would love her deeply.

Azaria would be proud—and that would be like icing on the cake. Starr's main concern was not if she'd find Victoria, but if she'd find her in time. Surely Astrid's days were closing in quickly now?

Starr returned to her laptop, mug of steaming Brazilian coffee in hand, tears still trickling down her tanned cheeks, until finally the words for her feature began to come to her.

Behind Closed Doors: For several months I have lived with the unbearable quagmire of grief that only losing someone you love with all your life can bring. My identical twin sister, Luna, was crushed by a concrete pillar in an earthquake while having the best time of her life, in Honduras. She'd found love, and was desperately happy. Luna and Patrick were going to have babies and live happily ever after. Our last Skype conversation had been about what bridesmaid dress I'd wear.

I feel like her death was my fault. If I'd stayed home instead of wanting to see the world, she'd never have felt like going to another country. Like our mother, Luna was a real home bird. I think her sudden desire for foreign travel was to prove something…perhaps that she was as capable and independent as me. I don't know if I'll ever be able to erase that level of guilt which weighs, like the concrete pillar that stole her life, heavy on my wounded heart. I'm so goddamn sick of the taste of salty tears. Enough, already.

There seems no way out of this pain. I miss her. I really miss her. Sometimes I feel like I can't breathe. It takes every ounce of willpower to gasp for air. I've had a dozen or so sessions, behind closed doors, with a specialist grief counsellor. Has it helped? No! Luna's not here. She'll never come back. No amount of talking about it is ever going to change this god-awful situation. I feel like someone has cut off my limbs, or ripped my heart out, and is expecting me to go on as per normal. Nothing will ever be normal in my life again. Never! I just want to scream. All the time! But I can't, can I? Society expects the grieving to take a few days off, and then get back on the treadmill like everyone else. But I'm not like everyone else. I'm not even like the person I was before. How could I be? My identity has shifted. Who I was just doesn't make sense any more.

Starr sipped the last mouthful from her mug, the coffee grounds crushed between her teeth like insects against a windscreen. A hot breeze forced its way through the screen door. She thrived on the weather in Western Australia, and her naturally olive skin—the same tone as Luna's had been, she thought sadly—relished the scorching heat. Later, she'd go swimming at the gorge with her colleague, Tobias. He'd be way more than a colleague if she'd had her way, but the rules of the newspaper office where she worked strictly forbid inter-office relationships. They enjoyed each other's company, and were often paired together on newspaper-reporting assignments: Starr, writing; Tobias, photographing. He'd been of great comfort when she came back to Australia following Luna's death, his bear hugs like a warm, comfortable, secure blanket. Starr valued every single one, and breathed them deep into her soul.

My experience behind closed doors has made me think a lot about people who spend their lives out of sight, whether because their occupation dictates it, or life's curve-ball has thrown them into a hospital or institution of some sort. I have contemplated the lives of various professionals, such as a mortician, mental-health care worker, psychic, funeral director, slaughter-yard worker. They would all have stories to tell, just as we all do. In a little-known world, unheard of to many, there may be secrets, classified information, confidential agreements, black-market trading, underground bestselling books, concealed affection, covert operations, forbidden relationships, off-limits agendas, smuggled wealth, and countless strange lives and experiences. At the heart, though, of anyone's story, is a need to be understood. Perhaps, even behind closed doors, we all need to have our life witnessed, even if the only one watching is The Breathmaker. In the end, no matter who we are, the only things left behind when we die are our stories.

As I start this feature, I'm not entirely clear who the people will be that I'll focus on, but starting with me, and my experience of feeling shut away, is a good start. I'm on the other side of the world from my family, and yet I feel that it is my family which will guide me towards the first person I'll interview. I suspect most journalists would plot and plan every last interview, and ordinarily, in the past, I'd have done the same. But I'm not that person anymore. I never will be. I've decided to approach this, ironically, not as a journalist, but as someone on her own journey. In many ways, like being behind closed doors, I'll be walking in the dark, not using my eyes to see, but letting my heart feel the way. My broken, pummelled, grief-stricken heart. My editor may not approve, but here goes!

Starr pondered her feelings for Tobias, and how, because of someone else's stupid rules she, too, was continuing to live her life hidden away. If there was one thing she was going to do before leaving Australia, it was going to be that she'd walk through a door. Determined to follow her heart, she completed her final two news stories for the paper, and then dialled Tobias.

A stolen evening in the Outback with him, camping beneath the stars — away from prying eyes, with no risk of being caught breaking office rules — their relationship took a path of no return. Starr relentlessly questioned herself. Her relationships had always been brief: Flings. *Fun*, she called them. She never had the time or desire to be in a serious or committed relationship. To her mind, commitment was like a prison sentence: Tethered to one person for a long time, your journey through life always within a certain parameter.

Without question, her career always came first, and there was no way in hell she was going to be tied down. She valued freedom way too much. Had this part of her changed as well? Was she, perhaps, finally ready to open her heart as well as her legs?

Countless stars flickered against the ink-hued sky on her last night in Australia. Starr felt different. It wasn't just that she'd defied office rules, but that she'd made a choice that was entirely at odds with how she'd always functioned. Tobias had proven to be her best friend, but now they were lovers. And yet, she was about to sever that precious bond by heading back to Colorado. Was she sabotaging the first good thing that had happened to her in months?

The Outback intrigued her, especially in the dead of night, for it made her realise she was never alone. Unable to identify the sounds of various animals, near and far, she eventually drifted off to sleep, peaceful, for the first time in months, comforted by the beating of Tobias's steady and reliable heart.

The vibrant red glow of sunrise, and the dramatic morning chorus of cicadas, kingfishers and honeyeaters, pulled the young lovers from slumber. *It's true*, was Starr's first thought when she awoke and saw Tobias smiling at her. *We did make love.* Something unfamiliar came to life within her heart that she couldn't identify. Smiling back at him, she reached forward and kissed his soft lips.

Reluctant to let her out of his arms, Tobias finally extricated himself from their embrace, and set to cooking their breakfast over the small fire. Eggs sizzled in the pan, and he added a couple of tomatoes. Their conversation was muted, both deep in thought about their imminent separation. The irony tore at them: *So close, and yet so far.* Lovers, at last, but wrenched apart by an outside force.

He understood that Starr had to return to Colorado. He'd have done the same. Selfishly, he wanted her to stay, but promised to be in touch each day.

They sipped Earl Grey tea, then tidied up the space around them, before packing up his four-wheel drive. It was a slow and reluctant journey towards the airport. Tobias sang along to a country-music CD as they drove. He knew it was her favourite song. He wanted to speak. There was so much he desperately wanted to say to Starr, but he could see she was holding back tears. Instead, he sang. This was his parting gift to her.

"It's going to break my heart to leave you again, Tobias. But I'll be back. I promise. I love living in Australia. This is my home now…but, for the next little while, my family needs me. And, I don't know why, but I've got a feeling that it might just help me with my syndication project."

He kissed her softly, sweetly, and one final time they hugged. She walked through the departure doors at Kununurra airport. Looking back, she smiled at him, standing there, so gorgeous: powder-blue eyes, soft beard hiding the dimples she knew were embedded into his cheeks, sun-bleached russet hair tied back in a bun. She made a snapshot of his face to hold in her heart. Deep within where no one, not even Fate itself, could ever take it from her. But she wondered, as she turned away, if they'd ever see each other again.

View from the Veranda

Isaac, Azaria, her mother Car, Astrid, and Bob were enjoying afternoon tea on the veranda, when Bob pointed out a vehicle beginning its ascent up the dirt road to this mountainside home. The Lafferty homestead had been in the maternal family for generations, and was crafted from local stone and wood.

"Expecting visitors?" he asked Azaria, knowing full well who the unannounced guest would be. It took all his might to not smile from ear to ear. He'd not even shared with Astrid that Starr was coming home for a quick visit, and that he'd assigned her to help find Victoria.

"No," Azaria said, standing up. She didn't recognise the car at all. "Honey, are you expecting anyone?" she asked Isaac.

"No, sweetheart," he replied, and then noticed the suppressed smile on Bob's face. *What's he up to?* Isaac wondered.

They watched studiously as the vehicle spent two minutes navigating the bumpy, unpaved road, leaving a trail of dust in its wake. Although the car was unfamiliar, the driver took the steep ascent as if they knew every pothole and rut. Azaria looked on suspiciously.

Bob walked down the veranda steps. Azaria looked at Isaac for an answer, then at Car. It was only when Starr pulled up in front of the homestead that Azaria realised who it was. She cried with joy and ran over to her.

"Starr, you're home! I've missed you so much." Azaria hugged her daughter tightly, and was surprised that, even with the short hairstyle, Starr was still the exact image of Luna.

"Ma, it is so good to see you," Starr replied, wrung

out and jet-lagged.

They held each other for the longest time, soft sobs uniting them once again. They'd parted with a baptism of salt, and were reunited with the same.

"I'm not home for long, Ma. Sorry. It's just a short visit."

"Any visit is better than none."

Starr took time to hug everyone, and they all returned to the veranda.

Over the course of many decades, the old wooden veranda of the Lafferty homestead accidentally became something of a ceremonial space, infused with the love and energy of family, friendships, delicious food, countless cups of tea, as well as tears shed both in happiness and grief. The wooden rails were painted white, and several pot plants sat atop the wooden floorboards. Beside the porch swing rested a cavernous basket with an assortment of blankets, all of which had been knitted or crocheted by hand. A large oak table, surrounded by chairs adorned with vibrantly coloured padded cushions, was often used for meals during the Summer months. They all gathered around it now, catching up on Starr's stories from Australia, and sipping lemon-balm tea, with dollops of Azaria's wildcrafted honey, from old pottery mugs.

Home. It felt so good. Already Starr could feel the internal tug of war. Home. Freedom. Travel. Adventure. Comfort. Family. Security. Love. Why did life have to be one thing or the other? Couldn't she have both? Couldn't she have everything her heart desired? Like, Tobias?

Eventually the conversation turned to the real reason for her visit: Victoria.

"Astrid, I need your help. I need to know every last detail of the time you had with your daughter. Are you up for that?" she asked tenderly, touching her aunt's hand. If she could help her in this way, it would bring so much healing to Astrid.

"I'm not sure I can tell you anything that hasn't been said a thousand times already."

"Granny Car?" Starr asked, "I know it's a long shot, but have you still got the photo of Victoria? The one you used to show us when we were little. The one you'd bring out each night at bedtime when we said our prayers?"

"Of course I have. She was my first grandchild. I was never going to part with that."

Astrid looked at her mother in disbelief. "You have a photo of my baby?" She cried softly into Bob's arms for a minute. "Mom, may I see her? Can I look at the picture?"

"A midwife called Sarah sent it to us. She said you gave her our address," Car replied, but wasn't surprised that Astrid didn't remember it given the state of grief she was in at the time. "I still have the letter she sent with it."

Car moved slowly to her bedroom, tears in rivulets down her crêpe-paper aged cheeks. Her long silver dreadlocks, like a royal crown, were wrapped up high on her head in a topknot. At eighty one, she was as graceful as ever. She had wondered many times, over the years, if this day would ever come. It had been one of the hardest moments of her life, to know her first grandchild was given away to a stranger. Car had desperately wanted to see that Victoria was safe, well-loved, and having a happy childhood. The unanswered questions had haunted her, though she'd never said a word or offered judgment about Astrid's decision.

Car sat on her bed for several minutes, looking at the photo. She knew every last detail of that baby's face, and had sent her a prayer each day for more than forty years, always hoping that the angels would deliver her message. And now, finally, the day had come. Action was going to be taken. That baby—now a middle-aged woman—would hopefully be found alive and well, and brought home to where she truly belonged. Wiping away the pools of salt water from her chin, Car cleared her throat before leaving the bedroom.

When she returned to the veranda—that sacred space which cradled her beloved family so faithfully year after year—Car passed over a handmade wooden frame. Inside was the image of a newborn baby.

Astrid didn't speak for several minutes. Her frail fingers ran across the glass inside the frame.

"She looks just like I remember her. You know, all these years I thought I was imagining a baby's face—a face that could have been anybody's baby—but I remembered her so clearly. Every little bit of downy hair, and that upturned nose. It's been with me all along." She sighed long and hard. "What was I thinking? How could I have let her go?"

"Don't go down that track," Car said. "You were traumatised and grief stricken by Rory's death. He sprinted into a blazing inferno to save a baby, and he never came out. You were 16 years old, honey. Do not blame yourself. When you meet Victoria, and tell her the full story, she'll understand."

"What if she doesn't? Maybe she won't even want to meet me?" Astrid choked on her words, the tears unfettered as they fell down her cancer-ravished body, soaking her jersey dress.

"One day at a time," Bob said, holding her hand. "Don't jump too far ahead, okay?"

"What if...what if she's not even alive?" Astrid sobbed.

The Maternity Hospital

Sunrise beckoned, and brought hope to the new day. Azaria and Isaac were up early, in the sunlit kitchen happily preparing breakfast together.

"I've made some lunch for your journey," Azaria said to Starr when she came into the room.

"Ma, what if I can't find her in time?" Starr asked, tormented by the possibility.

"You can only do what you can, sweetheart. Don't put pressure on yourself. Okay?"

"I can't help it. This is so important. More important than any job I've ever done before. I want this as much for me as for aunty Astrid. I desperately want to know who my cousin is. But…"

"What is it, honey?" Azaria asked, pained by the look on her daughter's face.

"I'm scared I'm looking for someone to replace Luna, and I'm terrified Victoria won't like me. I don't think I could deal with that."

Azaria had no words. She simply wrapped her arms around her daughter, and imagined that Luna was there, right there, in the kitchen with them, about to eat maple pancakes and sip raspberry-leaf tea. Breathing in the scent of her daughter, and holding Starr close against her, Azaria's gaze went beyond the flowering red geraniums on the wooden window sill, and down, down, down across the wildflower meadows where her four daughters used to play. She prayed there'd be a happy outcome all round.

The kitchen held so many family memories, and as the kettle on the red Aga came to a boil, Azaria silently gave thanks for the ability to nurture her family in the way she did best: a mug of herb tea.

With the remaining boiled water, Isaac filled a flask with freshly brewed coffee. He added it to the picnic basket Azaria had been working on for Starr. These women—this family—had become everything to him in the space of less than a year. He'd have done anything for all of them. They were his family now. Witnessing them as they struggled through grief had been the hardest part of his whole life. He had learnt, though, that each day was different, and that despite the pain, laughter had a way of sneaking in, as well as a subtle contentment. Life's small joys brought their own rewards.

"I was hoping to see baby Chandra before I set off, but it's best if I get on with this. Tell Bella and Ruby I want to hang out with them when I get back!" Starr said.

"I will! It's a shame you missed Ruby. She'd only just left to stay at a friend's house for the week, otherwise she'd be here and all over you like a rash!" Azaria laughed.

After tea was sipped, Isaac helped Starr take a suitcase and the picnic basket to the rental car.

"I don't know how long I'll be, but I'll call you when I start getting some leads. It's highly unlikely that Victoria is still in the same area." Starr looked at her mother, and at Isaac. They made such a gorgeous couple. Azaria, with her wild and wavy thick silver hair; beautiful, penetrating green eyes, and high cheekbones; and Isaac, with his full head of hair: a mix of silver and butterscotch, amber eyes, and a smile that had women of all ages melting. It warmed Starr's heart that her mother had found love again, and not just with any man, but an amazing one, who treated women as equals.

"Drive carefully, sweetheart. It's so good to have you here again." Azaria tried not to state that fact too often, but she couldn't help it. Life just didn't feel the same with two daughters living permanently overseas, and one...*dead*. Always, permanently, forever dead. She had Eliza-May living nearby now, but they didn't see that much of each other since she had started the job managing Isaac's shop: Appleseeds Health Store.

Starr switched on the local radio station as she made her way down the mountain. It was country-music hour, and she sang along with gusto to her favourite singers. She laughed at some lyrics, and cried at others, like the last song Tobias had sung. Many times over the years, Starr had wondered about becoming a singer-songwriter. She'd played piano since her toddler years, and learnt guitar at her grandmother's knee. Words were her passion, and her journals faithfully played guardian to countless lyrics. But life, sweet life, took her in a different direction.

The drive was peaceful, and alone with her thoughts at long last, she felt grateful Bob had called her. It was exactly the sort of mission she needed in her life right now: something to pull her away from her own feelings, and to step into someone else's world.

A few hours later, as she neared the hospital where Victoria was born, Starr pulled into a parking space beneath a shady oak tree.

Pulling out her spiral-bound notebook and pen from her handbag, Starr wrote:

> It's just a building. Red bricks. Large, white-framed, sash windows. Mature gardens. It looks beautiful. Here in the Summer sunshine, I feel oddly at peace. I imagine that for countless families this is a place of happy memories. This was where they met their baby for the first time.

It is true, though, that we don't see things as they are, but as we are. My mother has drummed that into me for years. Today, right now, I think I finally get what she means.

I can see the beauty and majesty of this building, but in my heart there is another story. This is the place where my cousin, Victoria, was given away at one day old. I understand the reasons for it, but it doesn't take away the haunted feeling I often had when I was growing up: knowing that I had a cousin, but that Fate kept us apart.

As a child, I would never have believed that it would fall to me to find her. And yet, here I am. Is this what every step of my career has been about? Working with words, listening to stories, finding answers? Searching, discovering, exploring my curiousity? I have a reputation for being relentless when it comes to finding the truth, but what am I opening up by searching for Victoria? Family is everything to us, but what if Victoria has no interest in any of us?

Starr thought about the song she'd handwritten when she was twelve. She'd called it: *Where Are You Now?* Before stepping out of the car, she sang it out loud.

After three hours of begging and pleading in the matron's office, Starr didn't feel she was that much closer. "I'm sorry, but Astrid gave away her rights when she signed the dotted line. My hands are tied." She apologised. "I really am sorry. There is nothing I can do."

Starr stood up to leave, and then she remembered something her mother often said when a person was only seeing things from one point of view.

"I respect that your hands are tied, Matron Caverlley; I do. Answer me this: if you were in my position, trying to find your cousin so you could bring healing to your dying aunt, how would you go about it? You know, if someone's hands were tied?" she asked, her eyes pleading for a glimmer of hope. "I just need…I need a door to walk through. Give me a door. Any door. Please."

Dusk lured Starr impatiently along the final road to St Maria's Convent, some three hours drive from the hospital. The Matron hadn't broken any rules. She hadn't actually said a word. What she had done was pull out an old tattered phone book and indicate that she was having trouble reading something. She wiped at her spectacles, held them away from her, then placed them on her nose again, shaking her head.

"Dear, could you just read that out to me?" she asked casually, pointing it out to Starr.

Starr wrote down the address and kissed Matron Caverlley on the cheeks. And then once more, for good luck, on her forehead.

"You will be richly rewarded by the Universe for your kindness. I promise!"

Starr headed along the curved pink-pebbled driveway, and entered through the heavy, black, wrought-iron gates.

"What a beautiful place," she whispered into the

evening air, feeling the cool breeze against her cheeks. Already, the mystery of the city-based convent enveloped her. Not one for man-made religion, Starr was surprised at how calm she felt, and suspected the daily rhythm of the nuns added to the aura of the place. *I suppose,* she thought, *if you're going to be stuck behind closed doors, this is a great place to be.* And then an idea came to her, quick as lightning. *Would Victoria allow her to include the story of her adoption in the syndicated articles?* Starr was both delighted by the idea and horrified to even think of such a thing when they hadn't yet met. The woman could be a tyrant. Best tread carefully.

Her boots crunched against the pebbles until finally she was walking on large, stone tiles. Chapel bells rang softly from the back of the property. Bad timing, Starr thought. Probably about to pray!

Knocking firmly on the front doors, she was taken aback by their beauty. Old, worn wood, studded with black iron buttons, the doors were majestic. *No doorbell?* She thought it odd. But her gentle knock had been heard, and a nun opened the door.

"Welcome to St. Maria's. May I help you?" came the lyrical voice of the young nun in her perfectly starched habit.

"Hello. I don't have an appointment. My name is Starr Linden. I was hoping to speak to the Mother Superior. I just heard the bells. I guess it's prayer time?"

"Dinner time," she smiled. "Would you like to join us? We're all just gathering in the dining hall. Down there, behind those wooden doors."

"I really don't want to intrude," Starr said, taken aback by the hospitality.

"Mother Superior has had a long day. Let her eat, and then I'll arrange for you to see her."

Starr smiled, and agreed. She didn't want to say

that Azaria had packed enough food to feed a whole convent.

She was seated next to a giggling trio of young nuns, and joined them in light conversation. When Starr shared that she had once interviewed a nun for the newspaper when she lived in Denver, their faces lit up. Yes, they knew the story. A copy had been sent to them.

Surprised by how delicious the simple offering of soup and bread was, Starr found herself feeling oddly at home. Her idea of a convent was that conditions were austere. And yet, here with these women, she enjoyed delicious food and lively companionship. In her mind she was having a conversation with Luna, and then caught herself. She was sure Luna was watching the whole scenario, a smile on her face as she cheered her twin on.

Mother Superior came up after the end of the meal and introduced herself, then invited Starr to follow her to the office. A mole on her chin featured several silver hairs which sprung out like a fountain. There were a number of pox scars above her left eyebrow. Neither of these distinct facial features diminished the glow in her smokey blue-grey eyes.

Contrary to the reputation of nuns in this position, Mother didn't seem at all cold or stern. Instead, she praised Starr. "Would you believe that everyone in the dining hall now knows who you are? That exposé of the poisonous leaks in Maryvale Convent that you wrote ended up making news way beyond Colorado. Well done for speaking up. The convent had tried for years to get the council to sort the problem, but it wasn't until your story hit the papers about those five nuns being hospitalised in the space of one week, that anything got done. Thank you. When you speak up for one person, you're speaking up for everyone. The world needs people like you, Starr. It's an honour to meet you. Now, what can I do for you?

Not trading journalism for a life behind doors are you?"

"No," Starr laughed. "Not exactly. At least not yet!"

"I don't imagine there are any stories in our convent that would be of interest to you. We run a tight ship here."

"And the food is fantastic," Starr added, patting her full belly. She liked this woman. Her eyes twinkled, and her humanity shone through. Starr prayed with all her heart that Mother Superior would lead her to Victoria.

"Many years ago, my cousin was brought here from Jaxborough Maternity Hospital. My aunt gave her away for adoption. I have no other details than that she came here. I feel like I'm up against a closed door. Can you help me?"

"We haven't had babies or children through here in years. *Years!* The convent often took in babies from hundreds of miles around, but then…"

"What is it?" Starr asked, disturbed by the look of sadness on Mother Superior's face.

"It was before my time. I hadn't arrived here, but had heard the rumours. In fact, it's why I took the job. I wanted to be part of creating a change here."

She stood up, the pain of the story causing her to catch her breath. "Something happened that caused great upset in this convent and forced everything to change." Mother Superior couldn't finish speaking.

Trembling, she stood at the window of her office, looking out into the courtyard. Her thoughts followed the wispy clouds in the moonlit evening sky.

"Things were different then, you know. Problems were swept under the carpet. Brushed aside. Forgotten… but rather like a nightmare you can't quite shake." Her hand settled on her belly, as if containing the contents. "Mother Superior died of a heart attack a few weeks later, but not before having put an end to this place

34

being an adoption home. All children in the convent's care were found homes, even ones who'd been with us for years. Apparently everything happened so quickly. I don't know if there are even any files from that time. Will you leave it with me, Starr? No one has ever asked about those children. Not in my time, and I've been here nearly thirty years now."

"Thank you. I can't begin to tell you what your help means to me. To my family."

"Where are you staying? How can I contact you?" the Mother Superior asked.

"I need to find a hotel. I'm not from around here. Can I give you my phone or email?"

"We have a little cottage down by the chapel. You're more than welcome to spend the night here. It's very simple accommodation, but I'm sure you'll be comfortable. I won't be able to start looking into this until tomorrow morning, and if you're nearby that will be better for both of us."

Starr couldn't help herself. She reached over and hugged Mother Superior. "Thank you. I'm sorry to have brought up such a painful story. I really am. I don't know what happened, but I can see how much it has upset you."

"Maybe it's time the story was told." Mother Superior sighed. Her eyes were watery now, as if holding the sins of others.

They walked through the convent gardens, and Mother Superior showed Starr around the self-contained cottage.

"Breakfast is at 7am. Please come and sit at my table." She bid Starr farewell, and headed towards the chapel to pray.

Starr looked in all the nooks and crannies of the little cottage, and then settled herself on the bed. The room had been tastefully decorated in sky blue, and would have been far nicer than the budget hotel she'd have probably booked into. With her journal on her lap, Starr began to write.

> I've been met with such kindness...women willing to help a complete stranger even though it goes against 'the rules'. I know what it's like to break rules, and the tug-of-war between liberation and fear.

Before falling asleep beneath the hand-stitched patchwork quilt, Starr skyped Tobias. It was so good to see his face again. She recounted her adventures, and that she was making some progress in the search for her cousin.

"I love you, Starr," he whispered after she had said her final goodnight.

She'd already logged off by the time she realised what he'd said. *He loves me?* Her heart skipped a beat, and her legs danced a little jig beneath the sheets. That night she slept as if everything in the world was perfect. And, just for now, it really was.

The chapel bells pealed just before five in the morning. Starr smiled as she remembered Tobias's sweet declaration. Breakfast wasn't for another two hours, but the only place Starr could think of was the chapel: she wanted to pray.

On bended knees, and aware of each one resting on the cool, slim, silk cushion, she bowed her head reverently. *Thank you, God. Thank you whoever is listening to me. I am so grateful for each step on this journey. I would love to find Victoria. Thank you for bringing all the right people, at the right time, onto my path.*

For some time, Starr cleared her mind of any thoughts, and just allowed herself the precious luxury of sweet silence. Afterwards, she relieved her aching knees, and sat up on the wooden pew as she studied the little chapel. Simple in design and décor, it featured an exquisite stained-glass image of Mary and the baby Jesus. The image of mother and child, bonded in love, made her more determined to find Victoria and bring her back to Astrid. It was never too late for them to be mother and child. Never. At least, she hoped it wouldn't be.

The Flower Meadow

Azaria and Isaac spent the morning pottering around in the flower meadow, tending the beehives, tidying up fallen branches from the recent storm. Azaria strung up a new line of Tibetan prayer flags, their colourful faces brightening up the field even more. Wildflowers swayed in the breeze, like ancient Egyptian bellydancers; and silent prayers infused the air. They hadn't had much time alone together recently, and enjoyed each other's company as they did little chores around the meadow. The beehive field was a world within a world, and Isaac had come to see how it was as sacred as any church. He watched Azaria gather an assortment of wildflowers. He supposed they were for placing in old jam jars on the window sills around the homestead, like she often did. But today she was collecting them to press between pages. It was a favourite ritual of hers to send them inside letters to friends, or in books she gave as gifts.

Along one edge of the meadow was a grove of Lodgepole pines. Beneath them, steeple-rooved hives, all of them painted in colours from natural earth-based pigments, proving to be a creative's paradise with symbols, murals and spirals adorning each hive.

Not for the first time, Isaac considered that the bees were given deity status by Azaria, and that the entire meadow was an elaborate outdoor shrine. There were conical skeps, too, braided from straw, and others fashioned from clay. Each hive was right at home nestled in a tangle of exuberant wildflowers.

As per her maternal family's shamanic beekeeping tradition, Azaria always spoke to her bees, being sure to tell them of changes within the family. Isaac left her to it, and continued tidying up broken branches for a while when he noticed Bob striding into the field. The three of them sat beneath the welcome shade of a juniper tree. Bob undid the straps of his dungarees, and slipped off his t-shirt to make the most of the sunshine on his skin. Isaac and Azaria were barefoot, their toes tickled by the long grass. They sat in silence for a few moments, savouring the warmth of the day.

"There's something I wanted to run by you both," Bob said, a little unsure of himself. "I hadn't planned to start work on Cottonwood Farm until after Astrid died, but…" he hung his head down. The idea of her leaving tore him apart. Bob wrestled with the angst. Sweat dripped through his salt-and-pepper chest hair.

"But she's still here? And time keeps moving forward?" Azaria said softly. She felt his pain. It was difficult living with her imminent death, wondering each day if today was the day.

"I'm in limbo. I don't want to wait around for her to die. As far as I'm concerned, while there's life there's hope! And, to be honest, she hasn't deteriorated despite being off the chemotherapy. Maybe those herbs you've given her are doing some good! We don't know how long she's got, but I can't help wonder if it might be good for her to see me starting work on the farm. Why wait till she's dead to help her with this legacy? Wouldn't it be amazing for Astrid to see the single mothers' home in action?"

Isaac gently slapped him across the shoulder, then wiped the sweat from his brow. This was surely the hottest day of the year so far?

"Sounds perfect," Isaac assured him. "Count us in, right Azaria? Anything you need, just ask. Building, gardening, food…just say."

"Absolutely. Anything at all. So, what's your

plan?" Azaria asked.

Bob breathed a sigh of relief. "I'm ready to start renovating and adding some new buildings. The architect's plans have all been approved. I can do most of the building myself, but any extra hands will be gratefully received. I'll need a plumber and electrician. Some of the electrics are pretty outdated. The place hasn't been lived in for years, and is really run down. But I feel excited about it. The buildings and property have so much potential. The property itself is amazing. I can't believe we got it for such a great price."

His enthusiasm was contagious.

Isaac asked: "How will it sustain itself, financially? After all, these young mothers will be pregnant or breastfeeding. They're not really going to be in a position to work."

"Exactly. One of our plans is to find ways for the place to be self-funding, and also for the women to contribute as and when they can. We'll provide food and accommodation and any basic needs like clothing and healthcare for up to twelve months. The idea is to create a single mothers' cooperative so they can earn some cash for themselves. When it's completed, we'll have twelve self-contained apartments, but I'm also building five small cottages so if women want to stay on beyond the twelve months and work there, they can. We'd like it to be a safe haven, and to give them the confidence to be great mothers, as well as to learn how to be part of a team for when they go back out into the world."

"How much of this is Astrid's idea?" Azaria asked.

"All of it." Bob smiled. "She keeps reliving her pregnancy with Victoria. Although she could never have imagined what would happen to Rory, she wonders how different everything would have been had she kept Victoria. There are so many regrets and what ifs coming to the surface for her. So many feelings she's kept buried for so long. I just feel if we can bring this dream alive — and, hopefully, find her daughter — then Astrid can leave this world with some sort of resolution in her heart. It's not too much to ask, is it?" Bob's heartfelt question tore through each of them.

"Not at all," Azaria said, her hand placed tenderly on Bob's shoulder in support. "So, what's next?"

"Well, now that I've got your agreement, I'll call the lumber yard and place my orders. I'm ready to start work tomorrow."

"Eliza-May pretty well runs the health store single handed for me now, so I can begin work tomorrow, too," Isaac volunteered.

"Would you like me to bring Astrid down during the day?" Azaria asked.

"I'd love that!" Bob seemed relieved. "If it's not too much trouble, that is. I want her to watch it grow, and change, and evolve. I want her to witness the transformation from something that's dying to complete regeneration."

Broken Hinges

Isaac and Bob left the mountain at first light to head down to Cottonwood Farm. The truck with lumber would arrive early, and they wanted to make the most of the fine weather. Bob showed Isaac all around the buildings, and what their plans were for the place. The possibilities seemed endless, and Isaac observed that this project was just what *Bob* needed, too. So much of his energy had gone into caring for Astrid that it was like being stuck in a time warp. Restoring Cottonwood freed him up to start living again. Isaac felt honoured to be part of their story. They moved wood, doors, and anything that needed replacing. A rather large pile of rotten wood began to accumulate, but in a short space of time the way became clear: this house would become something truly special. Like Astrid, it just needed tender loving care.

Bob thrived on the physical work, having spent the past year being rather sedentary. Isaac brought his old carpentry skills to life. He'd learnt the trade off his father, and had a lucrative career making bespoke furniture before changing paths and buying a peach farm in Canada. They made a great team, Bob and Isaac, their conversations always see-sawing between humorous and serious.

Azaria, Car and Astrid travelled over to the farm, and arrived by mid-morning to find the men hard at work, and more than happy to stop for a break.

Spreading a couple of picnic rugs on the grass, Azaria unpacked morning tea while Bob and Isaac helped Astrid into her wheelchair.

"Oh my, it's a beautiful piece of land you have here," Car said, taking in the view before her. "Simply gorgeous." She turned back to the main house. "Do something about that door, though, won't you?" she laughed.

Hanging on for dear life by broken, rusty hinges, the white screen door waited hopefully to be resuscitated.

"I have a door in the truck," Bob said. "Wasn't the first job I had in mind though. I want to make sure the floors are safe for you ladies to walk on. You might need to wait a week or so. Sorry!"

"We'll just have to bide our time, and take long leisurely walks around the property," Car said.

"Let's eat first!" Azaria said, motioning everyone to the food she had spread out on the picnic rugs.

They dined on raspberry and white chocolate muffins, and Isaac poured Brazilian coffee from the flasks, the rugged aroma of roasted beans infusing the air. Bob made a soothing chamomile tea for Astrid, and chopped fresh pineapple. The enzymes helped her digestion, which was still so fragile after all the cancer medication.

Isaac looked at the side of the house: three corrugated-iron tanks, flanked by a windmill. "Is that your water source?" he asked.

"Pretty much," Bob said.

Isaac looked at Azaria, prompting her to speak up.

"What?" Bob asked, observing their unspoken communication.

"Maybe Azaria could dowse and see if there's any underground water for a bore?"

"You can do that?" Bob asked enthusiastically.

"I can try. It's been a while, but I'm sure I could. The area here is so fertile, it's hard to imagine that you don't have an underground water source."

"Azaria the White Witch flies in again," Astrid laughed, her mocking tone not unnoticed. "Find us an alternative water source and I might just kiss you."

They enjoyed light conversation, and ate more than any of them should have, but it was great to be sitting outside together, enjoying sunshine and possibilities. The men finally returned to work, lifting rotten floorboards from the main living area, and replacing joists and boards with solid oak.

Car led the way towards upland pastures, walking slowly and mindfully, and Azaria pushed Astrid in the wheelchair. The terrain was far too rugged for the slim wheels, but the women were determined to see what they could of the land.

Located in the heart of a pastoral valley, the secluded farm featured panoramic views of the surrounding mountains and fertile fields. Hay meadows and upland grazing pastures eased out against a slow-moving stretch of a cottonwood-lined river which meandered its way through the 50-acre property.

The towering cottonwoods gave the farm its namesake, while forested mountains, aspen groves and verdant meadows belied the fact that they were just fifteen minutes drive from a thriving artisan town.

"I'll see if I can find some water," Azaria said softly, and as she did so, began to remove the citrine pendant from around her neck.

"What are you doing?" Astrid asked, rolling her eyes. "Don't tell me that thing is going to tell us if there's water under this land. Do you know how much a borehole costs to drill?"

"Indeed. We have a few on our land at home if you recall."

"And you found that water?" Astrid asked in disbelief.

"With this very pendant."

Car spoke up, "I know you're a sceptic, Astrid, but

give it a chance."

"I just don't understand how your necklace is going to find water. It doesn't make sense," Astrid protested.

"A lot of things don't make sense in this world. But we're not talking about the five senses. Dowsing is about using the sixth sense."

"Here we go," Astrid said, rolling her eyes again.

Azaria wasn't going to be deterred by her sister's ongoing cynicism. "Radiesthesia is a mystic art. It's an ancient way to communicate with the part of ourselves that is connected to All That Is. I use it all the time in my healing work to find the right remedies, and to detect health problems. Finding underground water uses the same principles."

"So what do you do?" Astrid asked, more out of impatience than curiosity.

"I need to ground myself," Azaria said, taking off her shoes. "This connects me to the earth and to my Higher Self. Then I can be open to receiving messages from the universal consciousness."

"Are we sisters?" Astrid asked, raising her eyebrows. "You're kidding me, right? You can't seriously expect us to dig an expensive bore hole based on a necklace swirling this way or that?"

Azaria closed her eyes. She visualised a powerful ball of energy at the base of her spine, and then imagined it going down to anchor her solidly into the centre of Mother Earth. She then pictured a ball of light at the top of her head, and in her mind said: "Open to the Universe now." Slowing down her breathing, Azaria aligned her thoughts to her heart area. When she felt ready to dowse, she lifted her pendulum. Holding the cord between her thumb and two fingers, the citrine hanging down, she spoke out loud: "Show me yes." The pendulum began to move in a circle. Using her other hand, she stopped it moving. "Show me my no."

To Astrid's surprise, this time the pendulum didn't move in a circle but back and forward in a straight line.

Azaria walked slowly, her bare feet tickled by the tender shoots of grass beneath her. "Is there water below my feet?" The pendulum wasted no time in swinging in a circle.

"Is this water fit for human consumption?" Azaria asked.

Astrid whispered to her mother. "Now that's a good question. No point having water if we can't drink it."

Again, the pendulum swung in a circle.

"Is the water fifty feet below me?" Azaria asked.

Instantly, the pendulum swung back and forward.

For the next half an hour, Azaria walked across different parts of the land, asking an assortment of questions. When she returned to Car and Astrid, who were both napping in the morning sunshine, she couldn't help but smile. Mother and daughter looked so peaceful. She understood Astrid's scepticism, but hoped she'd come around to the idea of putting in a borehole.

Azaria adored the feel of this land, and knowing the sole purpose for which Astrid and Bob had bought it, filled her heart with such joy. An outstanding legacy created from an old wound. *Astrid, the wise healer.* Azaria laughed at life's irony. *Light always creeps in at the source of our pain*, she thought to herself.

Making herself comfortable, Azaria lay on the grass, watching the clouds paint pictures. Her whole life, she enjoyed seeing what stories they'd tell, and what messages she could see. Of late, she had guided Ruby towards the art of using clouds as an oracle. She thought about her family: Kara, living in Zululand and working in an orphanage. Eliza-May managing Isaac's health store, and positively thriving in her new life away from New York. Starr was goodness knows where trying to find Astrid's daughter. And there were Ruby, Bella, and baby Chandra. Everyone was fine. Just fine. Everyone doing their own thing. Life moving forward. It was impossible to think about them without remembering Luna. Without fail, Azaria's heart always brought Luna into the picture. Where was she now? Was there such a place as heaven? An afterlife? So many questions. Many times since the horrific earthquake which stole her young life, Luna had visited Azaria in dreams: always there, laughing, smiling, so happy. It was both cruel and comforting.

"What's the crystal?" Astrid asked, interrupting Azaria's memories.

"Citrine. It's a quartz stone which is used to promote connection with the Higher Self, enhance psychic intuition, and is often used for drawing money. The ancients called it the merchant's stone. I use it a lot for cleansing a space, and for purifying and eliminating toxins, poisonous and negative things. You know," Azaria said, having an idea, "it's a good stone for you to wear. Citrine is ideal for healing."

Azaria passed the pendulum to her sister. "Here, it's yours. I'll show you how to cleanse it when we get back home."

"You know who you're talking to, right? World's greatest sceptic!" Astrid examined the stone, her poker face not showing a hint of admiration for its dark rich golden amber colour, and the natural sheen and lustre. She'd never admit it, but the thought of Azaria giving her something so precious meant the world to her. Maybe it would be a good luck charm.

"About time we check on the men," Car said, stretching her arms and yawning. "How long was I asleep for? More importantly, do we have water?"

Azaria laughed, tossing her long, silver hair behind her shoulders.

Azaria waited until they were back at the house to break the news. Isaac had set out their lunch on the blankets: artichoke tarts, olive and pepper frittata, tomato and basil salad with feta cubes, and slices of watermelon.

"Gorgeous feast, Azaria. This is fabulous. Thanks so much." Bob loved food. He was a strong man, and clearly needed refuelling regularly. No one could ever call him overweight, but he was definitely big-boned, and whenever you were around him, you felt safe. Like he could fight off a tiger. Or the whole world. Azaria thought: *No wonder Astrid feels safe with him.*

Sitting beneath the rays of Summer sunshine, everyone looked eagerly to Azaria.

"Well, the good news is…" she started.

"There's bad news?" Astrid interrupted, her face almost crumpling.

Azaria smiled, and continued. "The *good* news is that there is an unlimited water supply under this land. It's suitable for human consumption. You literally have enough water to provide a public water source."

"So what's the bad news?" Bob asked cautiously.

"It's 900 feet down. That's not going to be cheap to drill. However, if you consider bottling the water to sell you'd easily recoup your costs."

Bob looked blankly at her.

Isaac clapped his hands. "Fantastic. Bob, don't you know what this means? You and Astrid will be able to fund this renovation without it draining your current resources, and it means the home will be able to support itself financially for the long term, as well as create ongoing revenue."

Astrid's face lit up. "Really?"

"Really," Azaria said, hugging her sister. "This is

fantastic news, it really is."

Car was just about to say 'it's a good day to die', but caught herself in time. For years it had been her favourite saying, but since Luna's death she'd learnt to bite her tongue. She smiled, though, and in the silence of her heart declared it a good day to die. All was right with the world.

"You looked like you wanted to say something, Ma. What is it?" Azaria asked.

"That door!" Car said, pointing to the remnants of the old screen door squeaking in the breeze. "Let's pull it off so that Bob can put the new one up as soon as possible."

Everyone laughed at Car's determination.

"Right after lunch, Car. We'll make it happen today."

"I know you think I'm making a fuss, but a door says a lot about a place. And even though you've got weeks, maybe months, of work to do here, I think that a new door would give us a taste of what we've got in store!"

"We get the message, Car," Bob said. "What colour do you think we should paint it?"

The wooden walls of the old farmhouse were a distressed duck-egg blue with plenty of moss growing alongside. Behind the tatty screen door was an old red door. The paint was worn now, ruggedly blistered, and clearly hadn't been repainted for many years. A riot of orange and yellow nasturtiums hung over the doorway like a holy bower. An old terracotta pot, to the right of the front door, boasted a handsome lavender bush in full bloom.

Bob went over and removed the screen door from its loose hinges. There was applause from his audience as he tossed it to one side.

"I like the colours as they are," Astrid said. "A red door looks good and strong."

"Red can mean danger," Bob said.

"Or opportunity," Isaac suggested.

"It's the colour of blood," Azaria added, "so we can associate it with something positive or negative. In the end, it's not the colour which has importance so much as the meaning we associate with it. Red is love and passion and desire. It's romance, strength, courage and leadership. No doubt it's an emotionally intense colour."

"The colour of extroverts," Isaac suggested.

"In the East, red means prosperity and a long life," Car added, her wisdom gently mixed into the conversation.

"Red it stays then," Astrid said determinedly. "Red."

"I do rather like the red against the blue," Bob said. "Is this a good time to ask if we should keep calling the place Cottonwood Farm?"

"Too many decisions for one day, hey?" Astrid said. "I do like that it's named after all those trees down there by the river, but part of me is looking for something else. Something which really sums up what we're trying to do here. Does that make sense?" she asked, seeking reassurance.

"Of course it does. The right name will come," Azaria said.

Chapel Doors

Starr spent a week residing in the little cottage by the chapel, lost in a world of rambling conversations till midnight, over spiced-berry tea, and long walks through the convent gardens after prayer time. Mother Superior shared everything she knew about the years when the orphans lived there, and how it had impacted their little community behind closed doors. She often talked about her conflict between this life here, and a desire to be out in the world. Confiding in Starr, she shared about how she'd once been in love but had put her calling for this monastic vocation first.

Starr shared her own heartache: losing Luna. They bonded over stories, confessing loves and pet hates, and deepest dreams. Here, behind the closed doors of the incense-infused hundred-year-old chapel, Starr forged an unlikely friendship. It was one that meant the world to her.

"Mother, will you pray with me? I have to confess, though you've probably worked it out already, I'm not religious, but these past days here with you and all these lovely women have made me want to go deeper within myself, and to let out who I really am. I want to be a better person. More loving, more aware, more kind. Less selfish!"

They didn't bend on knees, or bow their heads. Instead, they held hands and walked out of the little chapel into the sunlight. Mother guided them towards the wooden bench by a small fountain in a secluded part of the convent's gardens; and they stayed there, hands entwined, and each prayed in their own way. Starr found herself not wanting to leave this sanctuary, but knew the time had come. She had all the information she needed in order to continue her search. It was time to say goodbye.

Later that morning, they stood beneath the shady trees outside the front gates.

"I'd like to come back sometime and visit, if that's okay?" Starr asked, hugging Mother Superior for the fourth time. As she opened her car door, she heard the words: "Our doors are always open, sister."

Starr nodded her head, smiling but crying.

"Always," Mother Superior affirmed, tears moistening her already twinkling eyes. "Now go. Go and find that cousin of yours."

Glass Doors

Another gorgeous Summer's morning brought birdsong on the breeze, and hope to the townsfolk, as Eliza-May opened the wide, glass doors of Appleseeds Health Store. It hadn't been that long since she moved back in with her husband James. Their daughter Bella was living in the flat above the health store with her baby, Chandra, and beau, Callum. Ruby had decided that she wanted to stay living with her grandmother Azaria and Great-Granny Car, for now at least. Family life had changed so much for Eliza-May, and she should have been happy. Or, happier. No longer was she in the grip of major depression. In fact, her days started with a skip in her step. Thriving in her new role as the manager of Appleseeds, she greeted each new day with hope and excitement, but something was nagging her... Ah yes, that was it. Now she could see clearly.

Her husband James had given up his high-flying career as a partner in a top New York legal firm to come over to Colorado and set up a small practice so he could resurrect his marriage. Life would be different, he promised. Eliza-May thought about that promise. Yes, he was here. That was true. And yes, they were living together again. But the harsh reality was that setting up a new law firm from scratch, in an unfamiliar location, meant he was rarely home before 1am. In the evenings, she felt more alone than ever. By day, she was surrounded by interesting people and lively conversations. Such a stark contrast to evenings pottering around the house and wondering just what sort of family life she had created. Fortunately, she was an avid reader so was able to immerse herself in other people's lives each night.

Alone, but not lonely.

Putting out two chalkboards that morning on the pavement, her face lit up when Clinton Hallett came by for his morning wheatgrass shot.

"Beautiful morning, Eliza-May," he said, unable to stop smiling at her as he stepped into the shop.

"Sure is," she replied, wondering about that increasingly familiar feeling in the pit of her belly. It happened every time he came to the shop. She fixed his drink, and they chatted for some time. Conversation turned to a book she had lying open on the side of the counter.

"Why don't you come to our book club? Come along tonight. We'd love to have you there. It's at my place. Number twenty, Chesterlee Street. Seven o'clock." Clinton smiled at her again, then said "Best get to work."

She watched him cross the street, then averted her eyes when he looked back at her, smiling. A few moments later, Eliza-May looked up again and watched as he opened the door to his bookshop: A Novel Idea. The shop had caught her attention early on when she'd returned to Colorado, and she'd spent a lot of time there at first, but she'd barely had time to visit since starting her new job.

The morning hustled by like a steam train, customers coming in for their usual orders: sage sticks, wildflower honey, incense, herbal tinctures and tonics, freshly grown sprouts, fresh vegetable juices, and Fair Trade gifts.

When Bella and Chandra appeared at noon, Eliza-May asked: "Would you mind watching the shop for a bit? There's something I need to do!"

"Sure, Mom. No problem." Bella had grown into motherhood with ease, despite being young, and nervous about the path which lay ahead. Surrounded by strong, caring women and men, she soon flourished, and Chandra's smile was adequate reassurance that mother and child were thriving.

Bella made herself comfortable on one of the shop's sofas, and then lifted her blouse and began to breastfeed, cooing at her gorgeous baby.

Eliza-May grabbed her handbag and disappeared down the street. Stepping into *Soul and Spa* was like entering an oasis. This boutique health and beauty spa was a one-stop shop for women wanting their hair styled, to have massages, reflexology or make-up. "I don't have an appointment," she said. "Any chance of a hair cut?"

"Yes, Mrs Megane. We can fit you in right now. I know how hard it is for the business people in this town to get time off. Are you happy to have your hair done by Julia?"

"Absolutely," she smiled, seating herself in front of the mirror.

Julia came along, expecting Eliza-May to have her usual request of 'just cut quarter of an inch, no more'.

"I want it all off. To chin length."

Julia gasped. "Are you sure? I mean, it would look amazing, don't get me wrong, but that's a *lot* of hair to cut off."

"I'm sure. It's time for a change. The women in this family all have long hair, and I've been rather inspired by my sister, Starr. Her hair was way longer than mine, but she cut it pixie style. I feel like she's really changed since having that done."

Julia laughed. "I can't tell you how nervous I feel!"

"Will you do my make-up, too?" Eliza-May asked.

"Of course. Are you and Mr Megane going on a hot date tonight?" Julia teased.

Eliza-May laughed, but inwardly her thoughts were nowhere near her husband. Why would they be?

Inches and inches of shiny mahogany-coloured hair fell to the floor. With each movement, Eliza-May could almost feel a part of her life being cut away. Change. It was time for change. Time to let go of who she was, time to be seen.

The transformation left her wondering just who the woman was, looking back at her in the mirror. For years she'd worn her hair the same way: one thick braid down her back. Every single day. Simple. Reliable. Easy. Predictable. She didn't want to be predictable any more.

"Wow." That was the only word Julia could say. "Wow."

"It's different, isn't it?" Eliza-May said. "I could hug you, Julia. It's perfect. I love it. Just what I need."

"Mr Megane is going to be blown away."

Indeed, she thought.

Another two hours passed, and by the time Eliza-May left *Soul and Spa* she did indeed feel like a new woman: her chin-length bob swished with each step. Eyebrows waxed, rosebud lips highlighted in deep aubergine gloss; she could feel a new persona emerging: a woman confident in her own skin. A quick text to Bella: *Won't be too much longer. Love, Mom xxxx*, and then she headed into Angelina's Boutique. She estimated that it had been about five years since she last bought new clothes. It was just before the depression really hit. Eliza-May was sure that those days were long gone. Never again did she want to exist in the pits of hell.

Two thousand and forty-five dollars later, Eliza-May headed back to Appleseeds. She was earning her own money, so figured that the amount she spent on herself was nobody's business but her own. As she turned the corner into Thorson Street, a skip in her step, head held high, and a smile on her face, Clinton stepped out of the bakery.

"Eliza-*May*?" His mouth stayed open, eyes wide in shock. "You...I nearly didn't recognise you." He shook his head. "You look..."

"You don't like it?" she said, worried that she'd cut off her hair and maxed her credit card for nothing.

"I love it! You look...*absolutely gorgeous*." Clinton kept shaking his head in disbelief. He ran his fingers through his dark hair, bit his lower lip, and said "Gorgeous."

Eliza-May noticed a flush in his cheeks as he spoke. "If you weren't married to another man I'd run away with you," he said.

He meant it as a compliment, but Eliza-May could feel her heart sink. She wanted to yell "What the hell has James got to do with this?" but thought better of it. It was best to keep her fantasy to herself. Of course Clinton wouldn't be interested in her. How stupid!

"I'll take that as a compliment," she said weakly.

"He's a very lucky man." He said the words slowly, but she knew what Clinton was really saying.

Their eyes locked, and when he smiled warmly at her, she felt herself go giddy in the belly again. Like she was fifteen years old.

"I need to get back to the shop," she said, realising she'd left Bella and the baby there for hours.

"May I walk you back?" he asked, his gentlemanly charm disarming her.

"Yes, I'd like that."

It was all Clinton could do not to link his arm with her.

As they parted, just outside Appleseeds, Eliza-May said "See you tonight."

His face lit up. "I look forward to it. Very much."

She breathed in his woodspice aftershave, which

57

lingered on the Summer breeze, before stepping into the health-food shop.

"Mom!" Bella shrieked as soon as she registered the makeover. "Oh my God! What *have* you done?"

"You don't like it?" Eliza-May asked, alarmed at Bella's hysterical reaction.

"I didn't say that. I do...I do! It's just... You seem like a completely different person. Not like my mother, but like some hot woman who has just stepped off a catwalk."

"Well, we both know I won't look like this tomorrow." Eliza-May laughed.

"Let me get my phone. I have to get a selfie of us to put on Facebook. Granny and Great-Granny Car will not believe this. They're still getting over Starr lopping all her hair off. What's happening to the women in this family?"

Bella took a photo of them together and then said "I'm pooped. Can I go home now?"

"Sorry I took so long, sweetheart. Really, I am."

"You clearly needed to do this...whatever 'this' is. Good on you! Mom?" Bella asked, concern all over her face.

"Yes?"

"Are you and Dad okay?"

"Yes, we're fine."

Seeing the Signs

6.57pm. *Tick. Tick. Tick.* Eliza-May shifted in the seat of her car. For five minutes she'd waited impatiently outside Clinton's modern brick house, tucked away in a tree-lined street, willing the second hand of her watch to go faster. 7pm Finally!

Clinton welcomed Eliza-May into his home, his beaming smile leading her into his lounge room, and then he introduced her to twelve other people in the book club. The evening proved to be thoroughly enjoyable. She couldn't remember the last time she'd laughed so hard, or had such interesting, thought-provoking conversations with strangers, and by the end of the evening it was clear that there were at least three people with whom she'd develop a friendship. Perhaps she could, once again, start calling this town her home.

There was something about Clinton's place that immediately made her feel comfortable: it was elegant, simple and beautiful. Nothing was out of place, and yet it felt lived in. Part of her wanted everyone to leave so she could be alone with him. She studied his features, imagining what it might be like to have some time together. Alone. Throughout the evening, they caught each other's eyes, both taken aback, and then smiled almost in relief.

As people said their goodbyes, Eliza-May picked up her purse and got ready to leave. "Eliza-May, could you stay for a moment, there's something I wanted to ask you."

She watched the others leave, and get into their cars. The scene was just as she had imagined. As they stood at the front door and waved goodbye, Clinton reached for her hand, and led her back inside. She looked at the hairs on her arms. Static.

"I thought it was just me," he whispered. "It wasn't until today that I realised you felt the same way. I don't know where this can go. You're married, and I am not the sort of man to break up a marriage. That's the last thing I want to do. But I know this: I am in love with you, Eliza-May. I have been since the first day I met you."

Tears, like medicinal waters from an ancient spring, trickled down her flushed cheeks. Could he really feel this way about her? No, she must be dreaming. She dug her nails into her palm, hoping to bring herself to full awareness, where she'd see the truth: it was all in her mind. But he kept talking, and she winced as the nails left their red telltale marks.

"I don't have any answers," he said, the truth in his eyes saying far more than his words ever could.

She looked at Clinton, his forest-green eyes so penetrating and soulful, grateful that the truth was finally out, and that they no longer had to deny their feelings.

"Maybe we don't need answers. Maybe…maybe a friendship is enough," he added when she didn't speak.

"It's not. Not for me. I couldn't bear it if we had to pretend that…"

He swooped down and stopped her from saying any more. That was all he needed to hear.

Eliza-May had never been kissed like *that* before. Were her legs about to give way? With the exquisite taste of him on her open mouth, she knew that she could believe in his love. He was there, right there, with her, and only her. He wasn't thinking about work or what to do on the weekend, or if the trash needed putting out. Clinton Hallett was an ordinary man who believed in life and love, and more than that: he believed in Eliza-May. He saw in her what nobody else had ever seen.

"Whatever is going on with us, I know this: it's a good thing. It feels right. I know the rest of the world would see it in black and white and judge us. But here—this—us: I believe in it. And I want more. I want *you*, Eliza-May."

For the first time in her life, she felt as if someone finally saw her; saw beyond the shy woman. So when he kissed her again, Eliza-May wholeheartedly fell into his arms and landed right there in his heart. And no one, *no one*, was going to take her away from that.

Leading her to the sofa, Clinton lit a candle and turned off the lights. Eliza-May had to chuckle at the irony: the threshold to her clandestine affair was being lit by none other than one of her mother's beeswax candles: famous for one-hundred miles around. She quickly put Azaria's face out of her mind. The last thing she needed was anyone telling her that what she was about to do was wrong. Nothing had ever felt this right. Finally, her tortured path through life was making sense.

"I'm not taking you to bed," he whispered softly, nuzzling her neck. "But I will. Of that, I'm sure. I want to know you, Eliza-May; all of you. I think about you every single day. I can't believe you're here, in my arms. I want to kiss you all night long."

She felt his words vibrate throughout her body. Her cheeks glistened beneath the tears. It was all she ever wanted in life: to be cherished. To be seen.

"I hope they're not tears of sadness," he said, gently wiping each cheek with the side of his thumb.

"I couldn't be happier."

The next two hours passed in a dream, their rapidly beating hearts disturbed by the strike of midnight on the clock in the hallway.

"Time to get back in my carriage, I guess. I don't want to leave."

"I'll walk you to your car," he said, disappointed their evening was coming to an end.

A gentle kiss beneath the oak tree was their final memory of the night. Eliza-May spent the ten-minute drive home thinking about Clinton, about the life she had with James, about her daughters, and about her family of origin. Was it possible that these emotions for Clinton were just an outlet for all the grief of Luna's death? Was she kidding herself that these feelings were real? Or was it because she was so desperate to feel alive after all those years pent up in her New York apartment?

Back home in her kitchen, Eliza-May fixed herself a cup of valerian tea. She knew without doubt that she'd have trouble sleeping otherwise. In a moment, she'd have a quick shower and then get to bed before James arrived home from the office. But that moment didn't come soon enough. He stepped into the kitchen, surprised to see her awake. "What on Earth have you done? Your *hair*? Your face. Your clothes! What the hell is going on?"

She was taken aback by his reaction. Was he angry?

"I needed a change," she said calmly. "I'm sorry if you don't like it, but this is my body." Eliza-May was not going to let him ruin what had been a perfect, magical evening. She stood up, carrying her mug of tea, and headed to the bedroom.

"I never said I didn't like it. You just took me by surprise. You're never awake when I get home, and here you are looking like you've had a night out on the town. I'm in shock. That's all. Come here, Eliza-May," he pleaded, apologetically.

The last thing she wanted was a goodnight hug.

"Good night," she said, slipping into the bedroom.

James followed her in, but already the door to the ensuite was locked. He could hear the shower running.

Twenty minutes later, she emerged to find him sitting on the edge of the bed waiting for her.

"What's going on Eliza-May? This isn't you. Please don't take it the wrong way. You look fantastic. Absolutely amazing. I really mean that. But you've always been a behind-the-scenes, shy, quiet woman. You've never been the sort of person who draws attention to herself. This new look…it says you want people to stop and stare at you. That's not the woman I know. I don't understand."

"Maybe I have had enough of being overlooked. Life's too short…Never mind. I'm tired. I want to sleep."

"Is this about Luna?"

"Good night, James."

With her back to her husband, she tried desperately to fall asleep. The valerian didn't even take the edge off. Her thoughts kept drifting back to Clinton's deep-green eyes, his kind words, the warmth of his skin. The way he touched a place in her heart, the coffee taste of his kisses…the way he whispered her name in the glow of candlelight.

There was no need, no need at all, for Eliza-May to be at work so early the next day, but she convinced herself that she could do with the extra time there to catch up on bookwork before the customers started piling in. The truth was, she hoped she'd have a few stolen minutes with Clinton before the rush. It also meant she didn't have to face James.

At 7am, she put out the chalkboards on the pavement. This was usually the time Clinton came along for his wheatgrass shot or carrot and ginger juice. She figured he must be running a bit behind after their late night. Eliza-May smiled as she relived their evening. She could still feel his fingers on her skin. Closing her eyes, he was right there with her, whispering, laughing, kissing. Every cell of her body felt alive.

By 3pm, Clinton still hadn't arrived. She stood at the front of Appleseeds Health Store and looked down the street to A Novel Idea. It was open. Customers were going in and out. A sudden thought hit her. Had he changed his mind? Clinton said he wasn't interested in ruining her marriage; perhaps the cold light of day had alerted him to exactly what he was walking into. Eliza-May felt her heart sink, and returned to her work. Maybe he was right. They were playing with fire, and someone would get hurt. This was a small town. If anyone discovered what was happening then everyone would find out.

The afternoon ambled by, painfully slowly. At 4.37pm, a florist from the next town arrived. Eliza-May's heart lit up. "Are they for me?" Clinton hadn't forgotten her after all!

"Are you Eliza-May Megane?"

"Yes! Yes!" She almost snatched the bouquet from the florist's hand.

She hurriedly opened the card: *About last night. I'm so sorry. You look beautiful. I love you, James.*

Eliza-May reread the card a dozen times, all the while shaking her head in disbelief. The bouquet was magnificent: pink lilies, purple hydrangeas, exotic orchids and more; and the scent, exquisite. In her heart, she knew she should be delighted by James's declaration. But the reality was that she was deeply disappointed that they weren't from Clinton, and that he hadn't been in contact today. What was she thinking? Of course whatever they shared last night wasn't going to go anywhere! How could it?

She placed the bouquet on a small wooden table in the reading area of the health store. It did look beautiful, and for a few moments she let herself feel gratitude for James. He wasn't a bad man. She simply didn't love him anymore. For some reason, she'd allowed her eyes to be turned to someone else. *Enough*, she said to herself.

She willed the big hand on her watch face to go faster. Deflated at the thought there would be no 'Clinton and Eliza-May', she couldn't wait for 5pm. All she wanted to do was go home and cry. Eliza-May grabbed the front door keys from the back drawer so she could lock up shop. The bells at the front door rang. *Not another customer*, she inwardly moaned, keen to get home and wallow in the accumulating pond of self-pity.

She plastered on a smile and turned to face her customer.

"Clinton?"

He was the last person she expected to show up.

"May I take you to dinner?" he asked, breathless from racing to the shop before closing time.

"I..." she looked down at her shoes, unable to find the words to express the disappointment she'd carried in her heart all day. "You didn't come by this morning. I thought..."

"I slept in! And then I had sales reps in all day. I haven't even stopped for lunch. We're good, Eliza-May," he said, surprised by the look of doubt on her face. "Nothing's changed, I promise. At least...not on my part. But I *am* starving! And I know my food will taste so much better if I have the pleasure of looking at you while I eat."

She laughed. They were good! *Good!*

"Okay, well I should go home and get changed."

"No need. You look perfect. I'll grab my car and be back out the front in two minutes."

"I'll be here," she smiled, hardly able to believe it.

Clinton drove about half an hour out of town, far enough away that they were unlikely to see anyone they knew. He'd arranged for a gourmet picnic basket to be delivered to his shop during the day. As they drove, it was all he could do to drive safely and keep his focus on the road. He wanted to look into Eliza-May's eyes, and never be apart from her. This was a new experience for him: to be so connected to another human being that the rest of life seemed irrelevant.

He turned down a dirt road, and just around the corner was a peaceful picnic area by the river. Clinton got out of the car first, and then opened her door. They headed towards the river, and set up a picnic spot.

Clinton removed all the items from the basket: wild-mushroom quiche and Greek salad; for dessert: coconut panacotta.

"Before we eat," he said softly, "there's something I need to do." Pulling her closer, Clinton sighed. "This has been the longest day of my life."

"Mine too!" she laughed.

"May I kiss you?" he asked, his words like a gentle breeze in her ear.

"Please."

They were oblivious to the children and families playing nearby. All that existed in their world was each other.

Azaria's kitchen was a hive of activity as they talked about the potential of bottling the artesian water on Cottonwood Farm. Isaac did some maths, and they whooped and cheered. Azaria and Isaac had been right: Cottonwood would be self-sustaining.

Bob and Astrid's business plan covered all sorts of ideas: an organic vegetable-box scheme; workshops to develop skills for young mothers: knitting, candle-making, baking, and more. Azaria hadn't seen Astrid look so animated for some time. This project really had given her a new lease of life. They spent hours that afternoon going through every last detail, and were confident that the building work would continue going to schedule.

The early evening was still warm, so Azaria, Isaac, Car, Bob and Astrid headed out to the veranda to drink iced ginger tea and enjoy the date and walnut loaf, warm and fresh from the oven. Car strummed her guitar gently, her agile legs crossed beneath her, as the porch swing went to and fro. Azaria and Isaac were holding each other's hands, and Bob was massaging Astrid's shoulders. There was a sense of excitement building as Astrid's dream came to life through their words, laughter, ideas, and hopes. Her dream became their dream.

Starr smiled when she saw the road sign indicating she only had another forty miles till she was back at her mother's homestead. The past week had been quite emotional, and she readily admitted to herself that she needed the stability of family. Laughing at the irony that her independent self even acknowledged that, her thoughts turned abruptly to her sister, Eliza-May. She wondered what the family had made of her radical new look. The reaction on Facebook after Bella had posted the photo was generally one of disbelief. Starr lifted a hand to her own hair. Still short, but now chin length, after cutting it off as a way to reinvent herself, she was sure that it had made a huge difference in her ability to go back to work. The last thing she'd wanted, as Luna's identical twin sister, was to keep reminding people of what they'd lost. Thinking of Eliza-May, she wondered if her haircut had anything to do with Luna. They didn't look the same, though they shared a family resemblance. Maybe it was more about their new start here in the valley. Starr wondered if James would ever have moved over here if Eliza-May hadn't packed up her bags and left first. Everything about their family was so different now, with them becoming grandparents to little Chandra; and Ruby living with Azaria. Maybe Eliza-May was feeling bereft of her children? Though, according to Azaria, she was thriving in her job as manager of Appleseeds.

Regretting not stopping at the last town for a break, Starr tried to remember what restrooms were on this route. There was no way her bladder would make it all the way back home.

She remembered a playground that her dad took them to years and years ago. *I wonder if it's still there?* Her memory was vague. It was more than twenty years since she'd been there, and her heart warmed as she recalled her father pushing her and Luna on the swings for hours. The only other thing she could remember was that there was a small café by the roadside just near the turn-off. If she could find that café, then she'd be able to make the restroom in time. It would mean leaving the highway, and turning off at Ploughman's Road.

A few minutes later, to her relief, she'd found the turn-off, then the café. And then, a small road with the sign and an arrow: playground. Starr pulled up into the car park. The playground was busy today with families enjoying the Summer sunshine, and taking time to relax with each other before school started again. Laughter filled the air, as did the smell of onions sizzling on barbecues. A breeze murmured through the willow trees. She thought of the irony. Kara would do anything to have a child, while Starr couldn't care less if she never had kids. For a moment, she wished Kara was here to enjoy the scene before her: so many happy families.

After visiting the restroom, Starr took another few seconds to enjoy the park. The Sun was thinking of setting sometime soon, and wisps of cloud, like dodgem cars at a fairground attraction, bumped each other across the sky.

Thinking of her growing feelings for Tobias, Starr couldn't help but smile at the lovers picnicking beneath the dappled shade of a willow tree: an attractive woman sitting on a rug with a handsome middle-aged man, clearly devoted to her every word. The woman was laughing out loud, her hand on his lap. Starr looked harder, her eyes squinting in the sunlight.

"It can't be. No. No way." If she hadn't seen the photo Bella posted on Facebook of Eliza-May's makeover, she wouldn't have made the connection.

She sat on a nearby bench, trying to process what she was witnessing. Was Eliza-May having an affair? Impossible. Never. Not Eliza-May.

Starr headed back to the car. As soon as she was inside, she got out her phone and scrolled back through her Facebook newsfeed to find the photo. Then she looked over again at the couple on the picnic blanket.

"No!"

Starr drove home, a foot on the pedal heavier than it should ever have been, and didn't even bother listening to music. What she had witnessed was incomprehensible to her. Eliza-May was always the good girl of the family: the daughter who did everything by the book, to her own detriment.

Starr couldn't get onto the homestead veranda quick enough. She had so much to tell Astrid, Bob, Azaria, Isaac and Granny Car, but this...*this* couldn't wait. She raced into the kitchen.

Greeted by the tantalising aroma of baked eggplants with melted crumbled feta coming from the Aga, Starr surprised everyone by entering unannounced.

"You're home!" Azaria smiled, so pleased to see her.

"Safe and sound," Starr sighed, falling into her mother's arms.

"Are you okay?" Astrid asked. "Is it bad news? Did you find Victoria? Has she refused to meet me?"

"I haven't found her, but I'm getting closer. I have plenty to tell you but I need to speak to Ma first. About something else. Have you got a minute?" she asked, looking at Azaria with a certain desperation in her eyes.

"Of course. Isaac, watch the dinner," Azaria said.

Azaria and Starr headed out to the privacy of the veranda. The Sun had set, and they snuggled up beside each other on the porch swing.

"Eliza-May is having an affair. I saw...I saw her with a man at the Ploughman's Playground by the Jessamine River. I'm pretty sure it's the guy who owns the bookshop. Clinton?"

"Are you sure?" Azaria shook her head, trying to assimilate the information. It was so out of character for Eliza-May.

"Absolutely."

"That doesn't sound like her," Azaria said, trying to comprehend the news. "I don't understand. She loves James. He moved across country to be with her. She hasn't said a word about not being happy." Azaria shook her head. "You must have mistaken her for someone else."

"I didn't, Ma. It was her. I didn't want to believe it. The thing is, I wouldn't have even noticed them if I hadn't seen the photo Bella put on Facebook. Why would she do this? Why would she sabotage her marriage? I thought things were good for her now? Didn't you say she was off her anti-depressants?"

"She *is* good, sweetheart, and, you know, maybe that's the reason."

"You're not endorsing what she's doing, are you?" Starr asked, alarmed at the possibility.

"I didn't say that. I'm just trying to understand. I'll pop down to the shop tomorrow and see her."

"Don't tell her I told you!"

"I am capable of being discreet, you know?" Azaria whispered, kissing Starr on the forehead. "Come and have some dinner. And…let's keep this between ourselves."

"I know. It's not my story to tell. I had to tell you though, Ma. I'd have burst wide open if I kept it to myself!"

Around the well-worn wooden kitchen table, Starr shared her stories of the hospital and how she managed to get the Matron to break hospital policy and reveal where Victoria was sent to. She put her fork down, more than once, and read pieces from her journal.

Astrid held Bob's hand tightly. Victoria was nowhere in sight, yet somehow, tonight, it was as if she were here in the room, alive and well, beside them all. Starr brought her to life with her word-medicine. Victoria was getting closer to being part of their world. Astrid could feel it.

They all laughed at Starr's stories of the nuns, and how they were just 'normal' women to her, going about their daily rituals with a love for the divine in their hearts, but as passionate about the concerns of the world as she was. She described the cottage she stayed in, and how kind the Mother Superior had been. And then, her face crumpled as she shared that the convent stopped housing orphaned children with immediate effect.

"I have the address where Victoria went to after the convent. That's my next stop. But it's quite a way. I'm going to have to fly there," Starr said.

"Where?" Bob, Astrid, Azaria, Isaac and Car asked in unison.

"South Carolina."

"Seriously?" Bob asked. "Let me pay for your plane ticket. It never occurred to us that she'd be so far away. All your expenses. They're mine. Just let me know and I'll transfer money straight away."

"It's not necessary, Bob. This is for me, too, you know. She's my cousin."

"I won't hear another word about it," Bob said firmly.

"Do you know why she was sent to South Carolina?" Astrid asked.

"Yeah, well, as I said, the convent wanted all children in homes as soon as possible and all the usual legal requirements were ignored. The Mother Superior died of a heart attack not long after that event. Victoria went to someone Mother Superior knew well: her sister."

"Her sister?" asked Astrid.

"Yes, apparently her sister, Bernice, couldn't have children, and was in her early fifties. The notes Mother Superior wrote said that she trusted Bernice with her life, and that she knew Victoria would be safe there. Bernice and her husband Steven owned a lighthouse in quite a remote area. I don't know if they still have it, or if Victoria is in that area, but I'll find out. After dinner, I'll book a flight."

"Thank you," Astrid whispered, tears falling, staccato, onto the table. "Thank you."

"My pleasure," Starr replied, reaching over and holding her aunt's hand.

Clinton reluctantly let Eliza-May out of his arms so she could get into her car and drive home.

"I had a perfect evening with you," she said, her heart filled with more joy than she could ever have imagined possible. "Perfect."

"I want to share my life with you, Eliza-May. Please think about how we can make that happen."

Eliza-May nodded, and then drove away. This was what she wanted too, with all her heart. Everything about her life finally made sense now.

As she pulled into the white-pebbled driveway, Eliza-May was surprised to see James's car there. He never came home early. What on Earth was he doing here?

Gently running her tongue across her bottom lip, Eliza-May could still taste Clinton's last kiss. Oh how she didn't want that feeling to end. *Who am I?* she asked herself as she slowly walked up the stairs of her home. Home? Her heart wasn't here. It never would be. Why was she even here?

From the kitchen, she could smell dinner. *Please don't tell me he's come home early to cook dinner?*

"Never thought you'd get home," he smiled, placing a tray of roasted balsamic vegetables onto the bench, then uncovering a bowl of chicken pieces.

"You've made dinner? Why? You never cook. You're never home. What's going on?"

James sighed. "Your haircut threw me for six. It really did. It was the wake-up call I needed. I have to get my new practice established, but I travelled across country to be with you. That's not going to happen if I'm always in the office, is it? I don't want us to get back to where we were before: when you were too depressed to get out of bed." He looked at her tenderly, his eyes pleading for her to recognise the efforts he'd gone to.

"Dinner looks lovely, but I've already eaten. I was with a friend from my book club. I'm sorry. If I'd known, I'd have made other plans. Anyway, I think I'm ready for bed. Lots of stocktaking to do at work. It's quite exhausting, really. Enjoy your dinner, James."

He watched her walk away. The realisation almost knocked him over: *he'd already lost her.*

"Eliza-May!"

She turned around, shocked by him calling her name so loudly.

"Please don't leave me. I couldn't bear it."

"I never said anything about leaving."

"You don't have to. It's written all over you."

"James…"

"Is there someone else?"

She sighed. The last thing she wanted to do was lie, but she also couldn't give him false hope, either.

"I'm really tired, James. Good night."

Later, when she felt her husband crawl into bed, she lay stock still pretending to be in a deep sleep. When James's arm reached around her, to draw them close together, she wanted to yell. She didn't want his arms around her! Not now. Not ever. There was only one man that she wanted to share a bed with, but how was she going to rip her family apart?

"I love you, Eliza-May. I always have, and no matter what choices you make, I always will."

She wanted to argue otherwise, but feigned sleep until eventually it claimed her tormented heart.

Out of Doors

Each afternoon, rain or shine, Bella would wear Chandra in a sling, and take a walk by the river. Afterwards, they'd stop at the park. There, Bella would place her baby down on a blanket and play the flute.

Azaria had stressed the importance of getting out every day for fresh air, sunshine, a change of scenery, and to bring some structure to her days. All these things would ensure she didn't suffer from postnatal depression like Eliza-May had. Some days, Bella attended a breastfeeding-support group, and other days she hung out at Appleseeds with her mother. For the past three weeks, she'd particularly enjoyed her stops at the park. Ivy, a teenager the same age, had been meeting her there. They'd catch up by the river, feeding the ducks, and quickly found they had a lot in common. Their conversations were often based on being a teenager in this town. Before long, it had become one of the highlights of her day.

"Have you ever read the Bible?" Ivy asked her that hot afternoon.

"No."

"Do you believe in God?" Ivy asked.

"Yes, I do."

"Do you believe in God's one true son Jesus who came to save us from our sins?" Ivy continued.

"Nope!" Bella was firm in her reply. Everything she'd learnt about God was from Azaria, and that was good enough for her, though she wasn't really convinced there was a god at all. Azaria was keen to teach her grandchildren about Original Blessing rather than Original Sin.

"God will forgive you for having Chandra out of wedlock. Would you come to my bible-study group with me? We can pray for you, Bella."

"Ya kidding me, right?" Bella stood up. "I like you, Ivy. I really thought we were becoming good friends, but I'm not going to let you make me feel guilty for the best thing that's ever happened in my life. Nothing about Chandra is bad or wrong. Look at her! *Look* at her! She's beautiful. Perfect!"

"But, Bella, don't you want her to go to Heaven? Don't you want that for yourself? You want to be a good mother, right?"

Bella shook her head, scooped up Chandra from the blanket, and packed her things away. "Goodbye, Ivy."

Bella almost ran home, and was so grateful that Callum was back from work when she got there. Tears, fogging up her eyes, and the words struggling to take shape, she finally asked: "Chandra's not a sinner, is she? Tell me she's perfect."

"Of course she's perfect. What's going on?" he asked, taking the baby from her arms and kissing Bella on the forehead. "What's happened?"

"Ivy said we were going to go to hell if I didn't pray to her God for forgiveness. I have my own God. I know having sex with Smudge wasn't the smartest decision of my life, but Chandra is the world to me. I don't need someone telling me that she's evil or needs saving."

"You really liked this Ivy, didn't you?"

"I thought we were going to be good friends."

"Come here, darlin', and give me and Chandra a big hug."

"I don't want to see her ever again."

"You don't have to. There's another park in town you can take a walk in, and there are hiking trails by the river. Or if you wait till I'm finished work we can go out together in the evenings to walk. I know you're on your own when I'm at work, but we can make up for it when I'm home."

Bella sobbed into his arms. "Everything has been so wonderful since I moved back here. But this...has really upset me."

"What would your gran say?" he asked calmly.

"She'd tell me to breathe!"

"Okay, so do that."

Bella giggled. "I wish she was here."

"Do you want to go to her place? I can drive us up there."

"Would you? I need her. Not that I don't need you, Callum, it's just that..."

"It's okay, I understand. She's a pretty special lady, that grandmother of yours. I always feel calm when she's in the room."

"Gran," Bella smiled when Azaria came walking down the veranda steps.

"Hello darling, this is a nice surprise to see the three of you."

But Bella couldn't contain her heartache, and sobbed into her grandmother's arms. Azaria looked at Callum, hoping for answers, but he smiled meekly, and then bounced Chandra in his arms.

"Cup of tea?" Callum asked.

"Kettle is already on," Azaria smiled warmly at him. She loved that he was already so well attuned to the needs of the women in this family line.

As they settled around the kitchen table, Azaria poured boiling water over a handful of dried rosehips and left it to steep for a few minutes. Out of the pantry she fetched a glass canister of freshly made cheesey oat cookies, and then placed several on a plate.

"Has your mother spoken with you?" Azaria asked, cross with herself for not having yet asked Eliza-May about the alleged affair.

"I haven't seen Mom for a few days. She's always busy with work or her book club, and she recently started jogging early in the mornings, too. Why?"

"No reason." Azaria's mind was racing. What could have caused Bella to be in such distress and turn up at the farm without warning?

"Gran, do you think Chandra is a sinner?"

"You know better than to ask me that question, Bella. We've had lots of conversations about this topic over the years. Of course I don't think that about her, or anyone for that matter. We're all just here to learn and grow. A wise man once said that we're all just walking each other Home. But Chandra? A sinner? Why are you asking me this?"

"I have this friend...I *had* this friend, Ivy." Bella started crying again, then reached for a tissue from her pocket so she could blow her nose. "She said that we'd go to hell if I didn't repent."

Azaria raised her eyebrows, then poured the tea. "Everyone has their own ideas about how this world works. If that belief system suits Ivy, then good for her. If it doesn't feel right to you, then don't give it another thought. There's no need to get distressed over this, honey."

"I knew you'd sort this out Mrs Linden," Callum smiled.

Azaria laughed. "There's nothing to sort out."

"The thing is, Gran, I don't want to lose her for a friend. But I don't want to be with someone who makes me feel bad about my choices, and about my baby. I love Chandra so much."

"Then you probably have to let Ivy go. Unless you feel strong enough to draw the line so she doesn't step over it again."

"I was pretty firm with her. But I feel bad for walking away and being so cross. I didn't want to fall out with her. It's not easy finding friends when you're a young mother. There are lots of lovely women in my breastfeeding-support group, but they're all about ten years older than me, and to be honest, I'm not interested in hearing about mortgage rates!"

"I don't have the answer, but I think you do," Azaria said kindly. "Drink your tea, sweetheart."

Car came into the kitchen after a long, solitary walk up to the beehives. Delighted to see her great-great granddaughter, and her great granddaughter, she settled herself down on a seat beside them. "This is a pleasant surprise," she said, smiling at Callum in gratitude for him driving the girls here.

Azaria relayed the reason for the visit.

"Is Ivy from that crowd just out of town, by any chance? The Barbican Reunion Cult?"

"What do you mean a 'cult'? She just mentioned her bible-study group."

"The Barbicans target teenagers and try to recruit them. Be careful, honey."

"I will Granny Car. I promise."

The Postcards

Kara's home nestled in the whispering tranquillity of a forest. The lodge was a chalet on stilts, and as she sat on the deck, the Sun rising over the horizon, the words came easily to her.

> I am finding deep healing here in Zululand. The orphanage children, despite the difficult start they've had in life, welcome each day with a smile and open hearts. The joy they bring me isn't something I can begin to explain. I have come to accept that I will never have children of my own, and that's okay, but I do know that I want to always have children at my feet.
>
> The shock of finding William in bed with another man that day has eased somewhat, I suppose put into perspective by losing our beloved Luna. My days have a beautiful, gentle rhythm, and I thank God for my wonderful life.
>
> I know you'll be happy with this news, mother: I am thinking of moving back to the USA. I came here to escape, and to be as far away from William as possible. Now I know that what I really need around me is my family. So, Colorado it is! I don't have a ticket yet. I'm savouring these last days and weeks here. This has been my home, and it probably always will be. I have no

doubt I will return again and again.

Is it silly to need my mother at my age? Well, it's true. I need you! I need Granny Car. I really have a deep desire to be around your wisdom and love. Love you, Ma. See you soon!

Kara xxx

Isaac came racing into the kitchen, desperate to share the news with Azaria. "Martin's coming to visit! He'll be here next week. I can't wait for you to meet him, and my grandsons."

Azaria reached around him, wrapping her arms tightly. "That's such wonderful news. Where are they staying? There's plenty of room here."

"I'll set them up in my house since I still don't have tenants, but I suspect we'll alternate between the two places. He hasn't said how long they're coming for. I don't suppose it will be for more than a week or two as he'll need to get back for the new academic year."

The Right Person

Bob was at Azaria's kitchen table, breathing in the aroma of her spiced butternut soup, and nervously tapping a pen against the wooden table.

"What's bothering you, Bob?" Azaria asked, placing the wooden spoon across the top of the soup pan, and tucking a frayed tea towel into her cotton apron.

"I need someone to manage Cottonwood Farm. I'll have my hands full with managing the property, and keeping the buildings in good repair. What we need, what *I* need, is someone to come in and be a mother-type figure for these women: someone with a kind heart to watch over them. It needs someone who can live on site and make it her home. It's more than a job; it's a vocation." Bob said, formulating more ideas for how the single-mothers' home would function. "It needs someone like you, Azaria. I know you can't do it, but you must know someone who has your nurturing touch, and is practical around the house and in the gardens. Really, it'll be a bit like being a dormitory parent, except the residents will be young women rather than children. And ideally it's someone who might have skills to teach. What we'd like is for it to become not just a residential home but a single mothers' cooperative so they can earn their own income."

"I'll have a think about it. There's a job for everyone, and there's always the right person for a job. We don't need anyone just yet, though. It wouldn't be until the buildings were almost ready, right?" she asked.

"Yes, that's true, but with Isaac's help I'm getting through the renovations quickly."

"Okay, I'll put the word out," she said, passing a spoon of soup over for Bob to try. She loved how he always managed to be around when she was cooking. His deep appreciation of anything and everything she cooked always left her smiling. That man was born to eat.

Astrid came into the room, Car pushing her wheelchair. "Fall is in the air. I can feel it," Car said. "Change is on the way."

The Lighthouse

Starr took another bite of her crunchy red apple, then tossed the well-chewed core over the ragged cliff, and watched it taken hostage by the crashing waves. Seagulls circled, their plaintive cries spiralling against the waves that pounded mercilessly into the rocks. Breathing in the pungent aroma of seaweed, Starr felt a sense of relief to have finally arrived, though it was not at all what she expected.

So, this was where Victoria grew up, she said to herself. The old lighthouse jutted out of the cliffs, but it was clear that it had been abandoned years ago. Wandering around, she noticed what would once have been a vegetable garden, walled to protect it from prevailing winds. A couple of old sheds, now partially derelict, appeared to contain a car and gardening tools. She breathed in the salty air, and took in the vast seascape. It was wild, remote and stunningly beautiful. Approaching the towering white lighthouse, she looked around to double-check there was no one around.

Surveying the red warning sign for some time: *Condemned building. Do not enter. Risk to life;* something about the scene broke Starr's heart. Victoria had been abandoned at birth, and then the place that had provided her with some semblance of home had been abandoned. Where was she now?

It had been a ten-mile drive along an impossibly bumpy dirt road to get here from the nearest town. Starr headed over to the door, rattled the rusty lock a little, and then with brutal force; and watched it fall to the ground. Unlike Eliza-May, Starr wasn't the 'good girl' of the family. Curiosity was her middle name, etched into every cell of her body. If Victoria had lived here, then Starr damn-well wanted to know what sort of home she lived in. She was hardly going to let a little sign with the words 'risk to life' stand in her way. Besides, they were faded somewhat now. She could always pretend that she couldn't make out the writing.

And with that promissory thought, she creaked open the front door. The first thing that hit her was the sneeze-inducing, thick dust swirled up by the breeze upon opening the door.

Entering swiftly, in case anyone witnessed her defy the warning, Starr was amazed to find herself inside a circular kitchen. Like stepping into a dolls' house, she walked around the room slowly, her fingers tracing the woodstove, the sink, the benches, the small window sill with views over the cliff edge. Sitting down now, at the dining table, her thoughts drifted to how the family would have lived here. How did they deal with the isolation? There was no question the seascape was spectacular. A self-contained person would probably thrive in such a remote setting. Something in the human soul would awaken to the reality that a lighthouse is the ultimate archetype for safety in dangerous waters. Is that what this place was for Victoria? A place of safety in a world which had been dangerous for her? A father killed in a blazing inferno. A mother who abandoned her at birth. A convent unable to provide love and security. Could it be that she was finally safe here?

Starr felt the sense of safety this place would have provided, its luminous beam casting out into the elongated, pitch-black, empty night skies. Without words, the beacon would guide mariners and protect them from danger. Despite the romance that Starr was conjuring up in her mind of this place, she wondered what sort of person or people could withstand such constant isolation. How many children, she wondered, were raised on deserted shorelines? What sort of adults did they become?

Deciding to take the spiral staircase upstairs, she was taken aback by some scratchings on the wall. She recognised what they were in an instant, for the very same thing was exhibited in her childhood home. A simple line, a date, and the name: Victoria. For four years, marked out every six months, Victoria's adoptive parents measured her height. Tears trickled silently down Starr's face. She was taken aback by how overwhelming she found the experience. Four years. For four years this was where Victoria lived. She'd spent 12 years living in a convent, unwanted and unloved. And then here, with two parents to guide and protect her, they took the time to witness her milestones. With a sudden gasp, Starr almost lost her breath. Each time Azaria had measured her, Starr wanted to be taller than Luna. Her whole childhood was a competition. She was the elder of the twins, and it mattered to Starr that she was taller. It all seemed so stupid now. If only Luna were still here, alive, she could be three feet taller for all Starr cared.

So, Victoria was an only child. Starr struggled to imagine what that must be like. In her home, it was always rowdy and busy and creative. At any given time, there'd be a sister playing an instrument, baking cookies, bringing in washing, helping their mother tend bees or gather herbs. In the Linden family, everybody else's life provided a soundtrack to your own. The emptiness that must have been in Victoria's life sent a chill wind through Starr's heart.

Grabbing a pencil from her backpack, Starr stood up against the measuring post and marked her height. She dated it, then wrote 'Your loving cousin, Starr.' It didn't matter that Victoria would never see it. But it did matter to Starr. It was a silent testament to their connection, and a visible promise that she'd keep searching for her no matter what. Somehow Starr knew that the Universe would find a way to send that love into her cousin's heart.

Slowly circling up the spiral staircase, and trying not to get dizzy, she came upon a lounge room. It was compact, with everything still in place. It was almost as if the family just left without taking any possessions. Despite the small size of the room, there were three bookshelves, all full to the brim. There were hundreds of books for teenagers and young adults, dozens of craft books, cooking books, and an assortment of maritime tomes. It gladdened her to know that Victoria had come into a home which valued literature as much as hers did.

It was probably an hour later when Starr got off the sofa. Lost in a daydream, she'd tried to put herself into her cousin's shoes and imagine life in this remote outpost.

Up two more flights of stairs, and she saw the parents' bedroom, and finally, Victoria's. She laughed to see the same Johnny Depp poster that Luna and Starr had had in their room. Although she was invading Victoria's privacy by being here, she figured that as no one knew then nobody could possibly be hurt. That was the storyline she kept throwing back to her conscience.

Feeling somewhat like Goldilocks, Starr lay down on Victoria's bed. The patchwork quilt, in navy blue, was embroidered with stars and moons. *Sisters of the silver Moon*, Starr whispered. It was clear that whoever made this quilt had done so by hand, and paid exquisite attention to detail.

She wasn't sure what made her open the bedside drawer, but before she could drag herself away, Starr's hands were inside, scouring the contents. What treasures would a teenage girl living in a lighthouse keep? There were pens, old packets of chewing gum, photos of the sea, a locket, an old notebook. Maybe it's a diary? Starr knew she was going too far now. Way too far! If she had any intention of meeting Victoria, then she had to stop prying. Or… But what if? Maybe?

As the journal fell open so easily into Starr's waiting hands, she expected to see pages upon pages of Dear Diary. Instead, she found guitar chords and song lyrics. *No way!* Starr laughed. *She likes to write songs too? Fancy that.* Her heart filled with joy, and discovering something in common just made her more determined to find Victoria.

But why didn't she take it with her? As she read through the entire book, Starr felt like she entered a new world: the soul of her cousin. Tears fell upon the brittle pages, and Victoria's early life came to light.

Starr knew it was theft, but there was no way on God's Earth that she was leaving that book behind. There must have been a reason Victoria didn't take it. Surely, wherever she was now, she'd want that book? And where was she now? Starr couldn't get that out of her head. Maybe she was living in another state, a handsome husband, a few rambunctious children, a job as a secretary. She laughed it off. Anyone who could write lyrics like that had a romantic soul, and felt things deeply. Starr hoped that whatever Victoria was doing now, she was living with passion and purpose.

Another flight of stairs brought her to the 360-degree observation deck. Her heart skipped a beat. The views were outstanding, and she felt like a queen at the top of the world. There was no question this outpost was hauntingly isolated, but the rich beauty spoke above all else. Starr imagined spending days, weeks, months, even, of her life, here writing. *No one would disturb me,* she reasoned, *and I'd always have the sea for inspiration.* And then, another thought came to her: perhaps she could come back here to write her articles? There'd been talk of the syndication being made into a book. Perhaps she could write it with that purpose in mind. And frankly, Behind Closed Doors would be all the more authentic if it were written in a place as secluded as this.

Day was ending, and Starr knew she had to get back to searching for her cousin. The last thing she needed was to be stranded in the middle of nowhere on a road that was no longer suitable for vehicles. Or maybe, she told herself, it was the very thing she needed. Mentally going through the supplies she had outside in her car, Starr made the radical decision to sleep in Victoria's old bed.

After several inquiries in town about Victoria, Starr was advised to see Mrs Tessany at the old Post Office. If anyone knew of people who used to live around here, it would be her. She'd managed the mail in this town for forty years.

The Post Office was housed in a white, wooden building with a red corrugated-iron roof. Starr headed up the veranda steps, and stood in the queue. For a small town, it sure seemed busy.

"Mrs Tessany?" Starr asked, even though it was clear from the woman's age that it had to be her.

"Yes, dear. How can I help you? You do look awfully familiar, but I'm sure we've not met before. I never forget a face."

"No, we've not met before. This is my first time in South Carolina. I'm wondering if you could help me. I am trying to locate someone who used to live around here. Victoria. She lived here about 24 years ago or so."

"Victoria from the lighthouse?"

Starr breathed out all the tension she'd been

carrying. "Yes!" she exclaimed with delight.

"Yes, she was quite a character. Expelled from school. Twice. She ended up being homeschooled. We all loved her though."

"Tell me more. Please."

"She'd cycle into town on that dreadful excuse for a road twice a week to collect her family's mail. She'd spend all day in town, you know, talking to each of the shopkeepers. And see that small elm forest over there?" Mrs Tessany said, pointing out the window to where the trees hugged a few park benches. "That girl would spend hours, there, with pen and paper. Goodness knows what she was writing but she barely lifted her head the entire time. A good heart, though. I was sure of that."

"Do you know where I can find her?" Starr asked.

"She left a long time ago."

"Where did she go?" Starr persisted.

"We can't be sure." Mrs Tessany's face lit up for a moment. "She won a guitar in a raffle one day. The girl would carry that instrument on her shoulders every time she came to town." The elderly lady chuckled. "Put a hat by her feet and busk the afternoon away. Not sure what she was saving for, but she learnt to play that guitar like a professional. Real fine voice, too. Never did know any of the songs she played, but they sure did make you cry."

Mrs Tessany filed some papers away before returning to the counter.

"What about her parents? Where could I find them?" Starr asked, desperate for a lead.

Mrs Tessany asked: "May I ask what your interest is in Victoria Lester?"

"She's my cousin. Lester is her surname?" Starr asked.

"Yes, her parents were Bernice and Steven Lester."

"It's a long story, but she was given up by her

mother, my aunty Astrid, and I want to find her. Astrid is dying of cancer and wants to meet her daughter. She wants to make peace. To apologise."

By this time, Mrs Tessany was in tears and desperately trying to wipe them away. "That girl has been through far too much. I had no idea of her early life. God bless her. The lighthouse has been closed for years."

"Why? Why hasn't it been taken over by someone else, or automated?"

"You don't know what happened there?" Mrs Tessany asked.

Can You Hear the Music?

Bella and Chandra were in the town library, and were packing up after mother-and-baby hour, when Bella was handed a flyer for a free musical performance.

"We hope you'll join us. It starts in about half an hour. There'll be free refreshments, too," said the handsome young man, who looked to be about the same age as her.

"Thank you," Bella said, reading through the details. "Maybe I'll come."

Bella strolled by the shops in the main street of town, and with nothing better to do, headed to a community hall several blocks away. Tentatively entering the building, Bella was awed by the warm welcome she received.

"Please come and take a seat, we're about to start."

The lights in the hall were dimmed as a huge spotlight shone onto the stage. A middle-aged man, quite attractive for his years, came out with a microphone in his hands.

"Do you want to hear music?" he asked, his charismatic charm working the crowd up. The audience fell into rapturous applause. "What about the best music of all?" Again, the clapping was deafening. Bella couldn't make out why everyone was so excited.

"The music we've all been waiting for is just a door away. I urge you to push it open. The music of angels awaits! I ask you again, do you want to hear the music?"

Chandra began to cry. The clapping and the loud voice booming through the speakers upset her. Bella lifted her blouse, hoping that Chandra would settle down and breastfeed, but she was too upset by all the noise. There was nothing for it. Bella would have to skip the concert and leave. Just as she was about to head out the door, a young woman said "Don't leave. I'll look after your baby. You stay!"

"No thank you. I don't leave my baby with anyone."

"I'm good with babies. She'll be just fine."

"Thank you, but I said *no*."

"We have a crèche in the side room. She'll be happy with other children."

"No thank you," Bella insisted.

Again, the man's voice boomed through the room.

"Young lady, do you want to hear the music? Come back and join us!"

Every set of eyes in the hall were now upon Bella. She was mortified, and felt the blood rush to her face. Why couldn't that damn woman at the door just let her out?

"Are you looking for answers?" he asked, staring right into Bella's eyes. "Do you want renewal? Then stay here. Let us help you find happiness!" The spotlight seared into Bella's eyes, blinding her and Chandra.

"Emily, shut the doors!" he ordered. "It is time for the concert to begin!"

Bella heard her heart racing. Did that man just trap her inside this building? She could feel a panic attack erupting. Bella reached inside her bag and retrieved her phone. Scrolling down through the contacts, she dialled for Eliza-May. But before the call could connect, Emily reached for it and said "Sorry, Matthew doesn't allow phones during concerts. I'll give it back afterwards. Now, are you sure I can't take your baby? You may as well sit and enjoy the concert."

Harp music began to fill the darkened room, and another set of stage curtains inched apart to reveal a small orchestra. "Do you want the elixir of the Universe?" he asked. Not once did his eyes leave Bella. Chandra was still unsettled, and not at all happy. "Do you want to hear the music?" he yelled. Bella had never felt so terrified in her life. "I can eradicate your moral issues. Let me help you find the way."

Somewhere between Matthew telling Bella she was the chosen one and had to eliminate the toxic people in her life, and Chandra's wailing cry, the baby was removed from her arms, and Bella guided to a seat. "We are your family. Through us, you will find salvation," his voice boomed through the speakers.

She felt herself existing somewhere between a nightmare and a hallucinatory experience. Bella was certain of one thing: she must have imagined what had happened. At the end of the afternoon, the orchestra packed away their instruments, and Matthew called once again "Did you hear the music?"

He left the stage, and marched right up to Bella. "How did you enjoy the concert?" He was handsome, and so charming, that she'd almost forgotten her earlier feelings of anger and fear. "We're so pleased you joined us. Do you play an instrument?"

"Flute," she said softly. "I play flute."

"Perfect. Come and join us tomorrow night."

"No thank you. I am a mother, and I can't leave my baby."

"Rubbish! We have experienced babysitters here. Come and play!"

"I don't want to."

"But *I* want you to. 7pm tomorrow. Be here."

He didn't seem as charming now, but there was something about the way he said it that made Bella wonder what would happen if she didn't come by. He just didn't seem like a man who took 'no' for an answer.

"I'd like my baby brought back to me now. I want to go home."

Chandra was fast asleep, and her little body was passed carefully back to Bella.

She left the building, stepping out into the glare of the sunshine as if walking into an alternative reality. *What the hell just happened?* she asked herself. Surely she'd wake up from the nightmare any minute now?

The Wild Storm

Starr finished sipping the tea that Mrs Tessany had brought her after they'd been interrupted by a steady stream of customers. Starr wasn't sure how much to confide.

"I went out to the lighthouse. Everything is just like it must have been when they lived there."

"There was a wild storm one night, and the light wouldn't work in the tower. Bernice and Steven were desperate. They could hear fog horns in the distance but had no way of alerting any ships at sea."

"I don't like where this is going, do I?" Starr asked, wanting to cover her ears.

"No dear. They carried lanterns and did what they could by standing at the edge of the cliff. There's an automated beacon out at sea now to keep ships well away. No need for that lighthouse."

"What happened, Mrs Tessany?"

"The storm was violent. It blew them down onto the rocks."

Starr sobbed.

"The coroner said they would have died instantly. Small consolation, I suppose."

"And Victoria?" she asked, sniffing into her sleeve.

"She was in the observation deck. It was dark, but she saw their lanterns tip over the cliff."

Mrs Tessany came around to the other side of the counter and held Starr in her arms. "I'm so sorry to have to tell you this news. I really am. Victoria knew she had no hope of climbing down that cliff, even though she knew every inch of that place. She rode her bike to town in the storm to get help, but obviously it was too late."

"What happened then? Who looked after her?" Starr whispered, tears in her eyes.

"She was 16 years old, and after the funeral no one saw her again. The government couldn't get anyone to take over that lighthouse. Apparently the story had spread far and wide amongst mariners. If a lighthouse keeper can't protect you, who can?"

"There must be someone who knows where she is?"

"If I could help you, I would. I know Bernice had one sister, but I believe she died a long time ago. In fact, I have a funny feeling that her sister was the reason Victoria ended up here. Can't quite remember the reason why. Steven was an only child. As far as I know, she had no surviving relatives."

"She must have felt so alone." Starr cried, her sleeve now wet from hearing Victoria's story.

"Can I get you another cup of tea, dear?" Mrs Tessany asked. "You look like you could do with it."

"You know, I think I need some fresh air. It's a lot to take in. Thank you for all your help. I mean it. Really, I'm just so grateful."

"I hope you find Victoria."

"So do I. Mrs Tessany, I don't suppose you know who owns the lighthouse now? Is it still under government ownership?"

"No, it was sold by auction some years ago, but as far I know the place has been condemned. And no one would dare risk their car on that road to check the place out. No one around here knows who the owner is. Sorry I can't be of more help."

Starr stepped out onto the street, taking in gulps of fresh air. What a nightmare. How could one person's life be founded on such pain? Starr thought of her own father's death: struck by a tree during a storm.

She didn't feel ready yet to share any of this information with Astrid. Drawn by the serenity of the elm forest across the road, Starr headed on over to sit on the park bench. *I will find you, Victoria, if it's the last thing I do.*

Scribbling in her journal, Starr wrote down every last detail of her conversation. She smiled to think of Victoria sitting here, writing music, pouring her heart out onto paper. She really was one of the family. For a few hours, Starr wandered through town, going into each shop, just as Victoria would have done.

"Can you tell me where the cemetery is?" Starr asked of the grocer.

"Sure, darlin'. Go up the end of this street, then turn left into Cedar Grove Road and drive for one mile. Not exactly the dead centre of town, but everyone's dyin' to go there," he chuckled.

She smiled at his attempt at humour, and then got in her hire car.

For a small town, she was surprised by how many headstones she had to walk past before coming to Bernice and Steven Lesters'. At the graveside, she recalled the words Granny Car spoke when they gathered for the funeral of her father.

Do not stand at my grave and weep, I am not there...

"I may not have known you, but I am grateful for you both. Thank you for looking after our Victoria, and giving her a family. I'm going to find her. I promise you that I will find her, and bring her home. She deserves that. Thank you for loving her." Starr dropped to her knees, unable to contain the grief within her. She was crying for Victoria, but she was also crying for her father, Jake. She was crying for Luna. She cried because she missed Tobias so much. And there were tears for Eliza-May. How could she just throw away a marriage like that? The last tears were for Azaria. She could really do with one of her mother's hugs right now.

As another day drew to an end, Starr contemplated heading back to the lighthouse. If nothing else, it was free accommodation. The thought of navigating that wild road, though, confirmed her decision: find a motel.

The Innkeeper

An old house, located on a quiet road, caught her eye. The Victorian Inn seemed like more than a coincidence, so Starr booked in immediately. The first evening there she spent sipping mint tea, and relaxing in a rocking chair on the first-floor veranda, watching horse-drawn carriages go by.

Cindy, a delightfully jolly innkeeper, brought out freshly baked lime and ginger cookies, and they got chatting about the folksy charm of the building. Starr had been rather taken with the braided rugs spread luxuriously across the heart of the oak floors. Each bedroom was decorated with brass beds, and featured antiques and hand-made quilts. Cindy let Starr know of all the tourist destinations in the area, and then left her to enjoy the ambience of the evening.

Starr spent five days holed up in her hotel room doing every conceivable search for Victoria Lester. She discovered that Victoria wasn't on a single voting register. There'd been no utility bills in her name. Nothing. Everywhere yielded a dead end. Was she even alive?

Once again, Starr was standing in front of a closed door, and she wanted to scream: *why is this so hard?* An unbearable thought occurred to her: *maybe I'm not meant to find her.*

She had utilised all her journalistic skills, and still she was no further ahead.

It was over breakfast the next morning: fried green tomatoes with crispy cornbread and lime-chilli mayonnaise, that Starr poured her heart out to Cindy.

"I just can't believe I've come so far to arrive at a dead end."

Cindy commiserated, brought Starr another tumbler of fig and pear nectar, and then sat down at the table beside her.

Although Starr had spoken fairly quietly, another guest at the next table stood up and came over.

"I'm sorry for eavesdropping, but have you ever thought that she changed her name? That's what I did as soon as I left home. I hated my surname: Piggs-Bottom," she said, the sarcasm spread out before them. "Don't you love parents and their ideas of double-barrelled surnames? My mother's odd take on feminism ruined my childhood. Maybe this Victoria of yours did the same thing."

"It never even occurred to me. Thank you. That has to be it." Starr spontaneously stood up and hugged the stranger. "Piggs-Bottom? Seriously? They called you that?"

The woman laughed. "Hard to believe, I know, but it's true. Margot Piggs-Bottom. But of course, school kids pronounced my first name as maggot."

Starr shook her head in horror. "No! What's your new name?" Starr just had to know.

"Lucinda Light."

"Wow, that's beautiful. Good on you!"

"I felt like a new person the day I changed my name. I haven't regretted it for even a second. Probably one of the best choices of my life, actually."

Starr, Lucinda and Cindy chatted the morning away, and then Starr excused herself so she could continue researching.

Her laptop before her, Starr stretched out on the king-sized bed. She navigated several search engines, keying in various details.

No, that can't be right, she said to herself four times in a row. *It makes sense, but it's impossible, surely?*

Heart pounding, Starr realised that continuing this search was going to be far more complicated than she could ever imagine. *Mahina Safiya*. She said the name out loud. The melodic roll of it on her tongue almost made her want to sing.

It was a name she was so familiar with, and she shook her head once again. Starr realised the Universe was having the last laugh. As she left the old Lafferty homestead that day in search of Victoria, one of the first songs on the radio was one she knew well: *Like Waves Crashing into the Night*. She thought of Tobias, and how he sang that very same song to her on the way to the airport. It had been at the top of the country-music charts for months. Both unbelievable, and making perfect sense, Starr said out loud: "So, I'm related to the great country-music artist Mahina Safiya! Sweet Jesus!" Without doubt, the hardest part of her journey hadn't even begun. If there was anything Starr knew about Mahina it was that she was a recluse, and never gave interviews. She believed in letting her music speak for itself. From memory, Starr was pretty sure Mahina still lived in Nashville. She'd look that up later.

Victoria Lester. Mahina Safiya. Wondering why she'd chosen that name, Starr started searching the internet for baby names. Mahina, pronounced, *mah-HEE-nah*. "Hawaiian origin," she mumbled to herself. Starr laughed out loud. "No way! No way! Meaning: Moon, moonlight. Hawaiian equivalent of Diana, Goddess of the Moon. Ma is going to love this! Astrid, not so much!" Starr kept chuckling. Victoria—*Mahina*—wouldn't have known anything about her biological family, or the importance of the Moon in the lives of the Lindens.

She typed Safiya into the search engine. Starr's laughter subsided. The name meant 'ocean'. Clearly there was a part of her life in that lighthouse that she wanted to take forward with her even though she was changing her name, changing her whole identity, and changing her life.

Starr headed downstairs and looked for Lucinda and Cindy, her face telling them everything they needed to know. "I found her. Well, I found her new name. I can't thank you enough. I'm going to leave now, but I'd love to keep in touch with you both if I may." Ever the journalist, Starr's contact book was actually several contact books.

Later that day, Starr made the decision to head to Nashville. Sending a quick group message on Facebook to Azaria, Bob, Isaac and Astrid, Starr wrote: *Getting closer. You need to know, though, that she's not called Victoria anymore. Her name is Mahina.*

Azaria replied within minutes: "Oh, the same name as that country-music singer you girls like?"

Starr kept her reply brief: "Yeah, something like that. I'll be in touch."

Autumn

Behind the School Doors

"What do you mean you're not going to university? Don't be ridiculous, Ruby. I can't believe how many times we've had this conversation." James Megane was at his wits' end. "I've been tolerant of letting you live up on that hill with your grandmother, rather than here at home with your parents where you belong. Now, when you go back to school tomorrow you choose subjects that are going to get you ahead in life. I just can't believe you've chosen art, music, drama and languages. Where's the maths? What about science?"

Ruby raised her eyebrows. "Jeez, Dad, next you'll be wanting me to become a lawyer. Why can't I make my own decisions? This is my life. I love school. Isn't that enough for you? Do I actually have to study things I'm not interested in?"

"Those subjects will not get you into a well-paying job or get you a degree of any substance."

"I don't need a degree, Dad. And, besides, all I want to do is with work with Gran. She's already taught me so much. I have other plans, too, but I'm not ready to tell anyone about them, least of all you."

"When did you get so feisty, Ruby?" he frowned.

"When I saw how much Mom's life changed by following her heart."

"What's that supposed to mean?" James snapped.

"She looks amazing, Dad. That skip in her step? You should be so proud. Don't you remember just how awful our lives were in Manhattan, or have you forgotten already? Mom has friends here, and a social life. She loves her job. That's all I want for me. To live in a community where people care about me. I have that here. Why would

I go away to university? Everything I need is here in this town. I'm not changing my subjects."

"Listen here, young lady. Enough of that. You'll move back here if you carry on like this."

"And you'd keep control of me, how? It's not like you're home most of the time. No wonder Mom goes out so often. She's just following in your footsteps, really, but instead of going to work late at night, like you do, she's with friends having fun." Ruby stared at her father, feeling angry at just how much her family had changed. "Are you jealous that she's got the life she always dreamed of? Does it bother you that she doesn't need you any more?"

"What the hell are you talking about?" James was so angry now, he thumped the table.

"Nothing. Nothing at all. I'm going now. Isaac is picking me up from Appleseeds in half an hour. I don't want to be late. I love you Dad, but this is my life."

The following morning, Ruby waited patiently outside the guidance officer's office.

"Ah, Ruby, come on in." Mr Jayne welcomed her. "I've been looking through your subject choices for this year. Do you want to talk about them and your future plans?"

"Yes, I do. I want to drop drama and do business studies instead."

Mr Jayne was taken aback. "Well, I must say, you've surprised me there. What's brought on this change?"

"I don't want to go to university or do any sort of formal education when I leave school. If I can, I want to understand what it would take to run my own business."

"And what area would you like to get into, Ruby?"

"I'd like a flower shop."

"A florist, that's fabulous. You know you can do courses in floristry at the local college."

"No, I don't want to be florist, I want a flower shop. I want to make flower garlands, and…it doesn't really matter so much what I want to do, I just need to know that I'll have some sort of qualification at the end of school that will keep my father happy."

Mr Jayne laughed. "Giving you a hard time, is he?"

"You could say that."

"Mr Megane spent years getting his degree and passing the bar. I imagine he's quite challenged by the idea of you not wanting to follow in his footsteps."

"Yeah. The pressure is on because my sister is a teenage mother, so she's not likely to get a degree any time soon. Ah, the pressure!" Ruby said dramatically, laughing, shaking her hands in the air. "Seriously, though, I'm really clear about what I want to do, and just need support getting there, because I'm not going to get it from my father."

"You're living with your grandmother, right?"

"Yes, I am. I have no plans on moving back in with my parents."

"Well, can I suggest you let her in on your plans?" Mr Jayne urged her.

"I'll think about it," Ruby said. "Thanks for your time."

"No problem. I'll get your timetable sorted, and you can start with business studies today. There's a class at 1pm with Mr Sellers. Ruby?"

"Yeah?"

"Good luck. Not everyone is so clear about what they want to do when they're your age."

The Barn

Later that afternoon, Ruby left her school books stretched open, like a wide yawn, on the desk in her bedroom, and headed over to the barn where Azaria was working. It was her favourite time of day: helping her grandmother label jars of honey, and make tinctures from herbs. They pottered around the work benches, the scent of honey, lavender and rosemary infusing the air. The radio was set to the classical station, and a Strauss waltz filled the cavernous stone and wood barn.

"When do you think I can be your apprentice, Gran?"

"When you've finished school." Azaria was firm but gentle in her reply.

"But I already help you every day. How much more do you think I need to learn?"

"Sweetie, I just don't want to get into a battle with your parents. Right now, your father thinks you're earning pocket money. You and I both know that if I dropped dead today you could easily take over this place. Don't be so impatient," Azaria smiled, bending down to kiss Ruby's flaxen hair. "You have your whole life ahead of you."

"That's what Luna thought, too," Ruby whispered sadly. "I want to make every day count. I don't want to put my life on hold."

Ruby's heartfelt declaration left Azaria too shocked to speak. Her granddaughter was right. None of us knew how long we had, and there was no point putting off the inevitable. Ruby wanted to follow in her grandmother's footsteps, and the several ancestresses before her.

"Okay, I'll start making your learning here a bit

more formal. But Ruby, just let your father think you're focused on school. The fallout isn't worth it, for any of us. And besides, your father has a lot on his plate right now."

"You mean with Mom?" Ruby said casually.

"What do you mean?" Azaria asked.

"I think she's in love, but…not with Dad. Whenever I pop into Appleseeds in my study breaks or after school before catching the bus, she's singing or humming. I don't ever remember her being happy like this before. Ever. I've only known her as quiet and gloomy. And that haircut? Wow. And every day she wears a new dress!"

"How would you feel if it were true? If your mother were in love?"

"Happy. I'd be happy. She deserves it. Is it wrong, though? I mean, is it wrong for her to be in love with someone while she's living with Dad?"

"Ah, sweetheart, that's one of the great conundrums of human life. We're not designed to be monogamous. It's a choice we make, and when we break that bond there must be a reason for it."

"Why doesn't she leave Dad? I mean, if he makes her so unhappy?"

"I don't think he does make her unhappy. I suspect he's just been so busy, for so long, that your mother felt neglected. It's easy for a woman to light up if someone takes notice of her. Women are like flowers, honey. We just want to blossom and shine, and have someone admire us."

"I want to say something to Mom, but if I'm wrong, I don't want her getting upset."

"Sweetie, you're not wrong. Follow your heart."

"You know? You know she's in love?"

"Starr saw Eliza-May with a gentleman up at Ploughman's Park. I haven't had five minutes alone with your mother to ask her. But even if I had, it's not any of my business."

"So you don't think she's doing anything wrong, then?" Ruby asked.

"I don't think it's a matter of right or wrong. It's a choice. I'm not in Eliza-May's shoes, so I couldn't possibly judge."

"Yeah, but what do you *really* think? I don't want the diplomatic answer, Gran," she said, putting her grandmother on the spot.

"It breaks my heart that her life got to the point where she moved onto a new relationship without making a clean break from her marriage. It would be less complicated for all concerned. I feel sad for your father, but I do understand how it got to this point."

"Even though he let go of his career in New York to set up a business here?"

"Yes, even though he made that sacrifice."

"Do you think he'll go back to New York when he finds out?" Ruby asked.

"Your father is an ambitious man. It's highly likely. I'm sure he'd be able to get in as a partner again at his old firm. But, his family is here. Even if his marriage is over, he has two beautiful daughters and a pretty cute granddaughter here who he can see every day. I think family love will overrule career."

"You seem quite certain. I think Luna's death shocked him as much as it did everyone else, and made him realise life is precious and short. It's odd, isn't it? That something so sad actually has blessings?" Ruby said.

Azaria held her granddaughter close. Life here on the mountain had changed so much since the Megane family had moved to Colorado. She could barely remember a time before they came here.

"Gran, can you do one of your beeswax readings? Can you do one for me?" Ruby asked.

"Whatever for?" Azaria asked. Ruby had long been interested in Azaria's ability to glimpse into the future by reading beeswax, but had never asked for a reading herself.

"Really, I should wait until you're an adult."

"Gran. Seriously? With all the stuff that goes on in this family you really think I'm too young?"

Azaria was reluctant. After all, she never knew what pictures the wax would form.

"We create our reality, Ruby. We're not victims of Fate. We shape our future by every thought we think today." Azaria had learnt the ancient art of ceromancy from her great grandmother. It was a simple divination method, but required years of study.

Azaria invited Ruby to sit on a stool across the table from her, and find a place of calmness within herself. She lit three candles, then switched off all the lights in the barn. In the dimly lit room, Azaria said softly: "Concentrate on a question you have."

Taking time to ground herself, Azaria sent a silent prayer to her Higher Self, asking for guidance about the patterns she would see.

She poured some water from the ancient spring into a shallow glass bowl.

Feeling within herself that she was ready, Azaria poured molten beeswax from a burning candle into the bowl of ice-cold water, and watched as it formed into shapes.

"What can you see?" Ruby asked, her eyes wide open.

"Tears. I see tears. Maybe there's a sense of regret about something. Maybe they're tears of happiness. I can't answer that for you."

"What is that circle?" Ruby asked.

"It means family coming together. A reunion, perhaps."

"You're being vague, Gran. This is *me* you're reading for. You don't have to hide anything."

"Ruby, the future is not set in stone, or wax, for that matter. We have a choice, every single day, what direction to go in."

"Yes, I know that, but I want to know what is ahead of me for the next year or so."

Feeling pincered by Ruby's determination, Azaria took a long, deep breath.

"I see tremendous sorrow, but we both know that Astrid isn't for this world for much longer, so I'm not really divining anything either of us don't already know."

"Maybe it's someone else. If we know about Astrid then there's no reason for it to show up, is there?"

Azaria was regretting ever being talked into this. She knew that it wasn't about Astrid. And she didn't think it was about Car, either. For some reason, she couldn't get Eliza-May out of her head. It didn't make sense, though, because she was so happy.

"Hey, look at this heart. I see love. Is there a boy you've got a crush on Ruby?"

"That's in there? YES!" Ruby stood up, clapped her hands, and hugged Azaria. Her face, flushed like raspberry sorbet, said everything Azaria sensed.

"That's all I wanted to know. Thanks! I'm going to go and do some more homework. Love you, Gran."

Azaria laughed. Ruby in love. Oh dear. And she reckoned she was going to do homework?

Ruby thrived on living at the farm, and particularly enjoyed evening mealtimes in the old Lafferty homestead. Each night, Bob would come in from working at Cottonwood Farm with Isaac, exhausted from their building and renovation; and Azaria and Car would bring dinner to the large oak table. Astrid would sit in her wheelchair, reading a book, the cat snuggled firmly on the crocheted blanket stretched across her lap. Whether it was the attention and care brought to each meal, or the laughter, or the adult conversations about things Ruby found eternally fascinating, she soaked up the atmosphere. And the love. Especially the love. It was also the first time in her life that she got to be an only child, and was nowhere near ready to give that up. Having five adults doting on her, and showing genuine interest in her, and her studies, filled her with a determination to create the life of her dreams: just as Azaria had done.

Ruby chatted with Isaac while they washed and dried the dishes. He was always interested to hear about her greatest love of all: flowers. They talked about how she listened to life, and Ruby confided that she felt she only had to ask a question and a voice would answer it.

"Could be that you're clairaudient," he said, putting the chequered tea towel on the bench.

"What's that?" she asked, curiously.

"It could be your spirit guides talking to you, or an angel. Maybe it's even a deceased relative."

"Oh yeah, well, Luna talks to me all the time!" Ruby beamed with delight.

Car, still in the kitchen, tidying up the cat bowl, overheard. "Does she, Ruby?"

"Yeah," she said, her casual tone indicative of how she took these otherworld conversations for granted.

"Why have you never shared that before?" Car asked.

"They're private conversations. She tells me stuff. Stuff that's happening in the family."

Car smiled. That's all she needed to know: that Luna was still with them. Still loving them all. Not that Car ever had any doubt.

Isaac continued, "Some clairaudients hear music, others hear phrases, and some hear certain sounds."

"Well, when Luna speaks, it's in full-on sentences. You know, she's way more talkative than Starr, and I never knew that when she was alive."

Isaac laughed, but was desperate for Azaria to hear the conversation. She was sorting out laundry and putting clothes away.

"The thing that annoys me, though, is that I only get messages to do with other people, and not myself."

Azaria carried the weathered woven-willow basket on her hip, just as she had done for decades, and placed Ruby's neatly folded clothes onto the bed. As she headed out of the room, the books on Ruby's desk caught her eye. Business studies? Business text books? Azaria shook her head. It didn't make sense. Ruby was doing arts and music, not business. Had James put her up to this?

By the time Azaria had returned to the kitchen, Isaac was steeping lemon-balm tea. Ruby, scouting through the pantry on a hunt for maple and ginger cookies, exclaimed "Oh my God, Gran has made chocolate cake. Why didn't she tell me there was chocolate cake?"

Azaria laughed. "It was meant to be a surprise. Go on then, get it out."

Ruby brought the cake tin to the table, her smile contagious.

"You can take a couple of pieces over to the loft for Bob and Astrid."

"Before I have mine or after?" Ruby asked, licking the icing off her fingers.

"Before!" Isaac replied, laughing as he put his arms

around Azaria's waist.

"Okay," she said, then placed two slices onto a plate and headed out the kitchen.

"Don't bang the door!" Azaria and Isaac called out in unison when she stepped onto the veranda. But it was too late.

"Did she say anything to you about doing business studies?" Azaria asked Car.

"Business studies? Ruby?" Car was perplexed.

"Yes. She's got business books on her desk, and is doing homework sheets. Eliza-May didn't mention anything."

"She was talking the other day," Isaac interrupted, "about having a shop when she leaves school. She was actually trying to convince me to buy the old shop next to Appleseeds. You know, that tiny, run-down old barber's shop. Said it would be perfect for what she had in mind."

"And what on Earth does she have in mind?" Azaria asked.

"Didn't say, just mumbled something about time waits for no woman."

The three of them laughed. Ruby was most certainly one of a kind.

When she returned, skipping into the kitchen, a telltale smudge of chocolate icing across her lips, Azaria brought up the subject.

"I couldn't help notice you've got some business textbooks on your desk. Anything you want to share with us, Rubes?"

"No, not yet." She sat down, and consumed her cake as if it were her last supper. Azaria was surprised she could fit it in given how much dinner she'd eaten, and that Astrid had probably palmed off her cake to Ruby.

Azaria knew better than to push any subject with

Ruby. She'd speak when the time was right.

"Best you finish your homework and get ready for bed," Azaria suggested.

"Can I take a piece of cake to school tomorrow? It's really good!" Ruby asked, eyeing up the last piece.

"You mean two pieces weren't enough?" Isaac laughed.

"How did you know Astrid gave me hers?" Ruby's eyes grew wide. "I ate it while I was over there. Are you psychic?" she demanded to know.

Car giggled. "You need to hide the evidence better next time. You had icing all over your mouth."

Scrunching up her lips and frowning, Ruby rinsed her plate at the sink, then headed off to her bedroom.

"Good night," she said, her words barely a whisper.

"We love you, Rubes!" Azaria called out after her, trying to contain her laughter. "I'll come and tuck you in bed in a jiffy."

"I think I'm ready for bed. It's been a long day. Will I see you soon?" Azaria asked Isaac, and then kissed Car goodnight.

"I'll be right there," he replied.

Isaac crawled into bed, watching Azaria as she did her obligatory 100 strokes with the hairbrush. She could see his reflection in the mirror.

"Why are you smiling?" she asked, then turned around to look at him. She never tired of the view: his silver-butterscotch hair and amber eyes, set against a healthy tan and lean muscle, belied his age. It was his smile. Like the sky, it was always there, ready to open her heart.

"I overheard a conversation at Appleseeds today between two regular customers. You know them: Mrs Symes and Cath Cullocks," said Isaac. "They were talking about how beautiful you are, and wondering about your secrets to looking good."

"And what did you tell them?" Azaria asked.

"They didn't know I was eavesdropping! But, if I had been asked for an opinion, I'd tell them this: There's not a day goes by where you don't honour your body and your mind and your emotions. I watch you brush your sparkly silver hair each evening, and you give it the same care and devotion as if you were tending your bees or nurturing your herb gardens or loving that beautiful great-granddaughter of yours. In all the time I've known you, I've only witnessed you be kind to yourself, even on the worst of days."

"Even when Luna died?" she queried.

"Even then. *Especially* then. I heard you that night after we placed her on the bed; you were outside under the stars, giving thanks for your children, your mother, and…for me. Sure, you'd spent the afternoon screaming, but that was a necessary part of dealing with the shock of what happened. What you spoke to the stars or the Moon or the Goddess, whoever it was you were engaged with, well… I don't think there's a church in the world that could make me feel as if I were on more sacred ground than I did that night."

"Thank you, Isaac. Sometimes it's only through another's eyes that we really see ourselves."

"Well, that's the thing. I think you *do* see yourself. That's my point, really. I've never known a woman like you before. A woman who can look at herself in the mirror and not complain about her nose or her crooked chin or wrinkly lines."

"Do I have a crooked chin?" she asked.

"No," Isaac laughed. "Now, if you don't mind, I'd like to merge with that mesmerising creature I see before me. Are you ready for bed yet?"

"Hmmmm, you should know by now that there are a few more things I do after brushing my hair."

"Of course I do. You light this candle, brush your teeth, massage your home-made moisturiser across every inch of your glorious body, then you sprinkle lavender oil on your pillow. When you crawl into bed, you write for a few minutes in your gratitude journal. But, honey, I could well be asleep by then. All that building work I'm doing most days is meant for young men. I'm worn out."

She walked over to her bedside table, and lit two beeswax candles.

Azaria slipped off her dress and let it fall to the floor.

"Goodnight then," she smiled cheekily, and stepped into the en suite to brush her teeth. *Ah well, if he's that tired, I might as well have a shower*, she thought, turning it on full.

Standing beneath the powerful jet of steamy water, she sighed as she washed the day away. "Thank you for everything," she said softly, her declaration of gratitude to a divine force spoken with reverence.

"You're welcome," Isaac smiled, stepping in the shower beside her.

"Thought you were tired?" Azaria whispered as his arms came around her waist, and he kissed her shoulder.

"Did you really think that I was going to fall asleep after seeing you standing there, naked, by candlelight?"

A Novel Idea

Clinton was talking to two of his staff members when the gentleman who'd just arrived through the front door caught his eye: James Megane. Dressed in his Armani suit and shiny leather shoes, James was a formidable and imposing man who had clearly commanded respect the moment he moved to town and opened up his own law firm. His reputation as a leading Manhattan attorney had preceded him.

The first thing Clinton noticed was that his hands were sweating, and his heart began to race. Had Eliza-May told James of their 'friendship'? Or, had James worked it out for himself? Surprised to see the town's new lawyer simply browsing the shelves, Clinton busied himself behind the counter, watching James's every move through the store's closed-circuit television. If James was interested in confronting Clinton, he sure was taking his time about it.

Although James and Clinton had never met, they were both aware of who the other man was. Clinton had run the bookshop successfully for many years, and was loved and admired around town.

James gathered up three books, and then headed to the main counter, where he was served by Savannah, a new staff member. As she processed his order, she asked him if he'd like the books gift wrapped. She figured that as they were all from the women's fiction area, they were unlikely to be for him.

"That would be great, thank you," he said, not making eye contact. Instead, he read through a flyer which lay on the counter: *Weekly Bookclub. New members welcome.*

"My wife goes to this book club. Do many people go along?"

"Yes, there's quite a big group now. Mr Hallett, how many go to your book club now?"

Clinton could have kicked her, but took a deep breath and turned to face James.

"Hi. There are about a dozen of us."

"Would you mind if I come along? It might be nice to share this with my wife."

Clinton's heart hit the floor, like an egg cracking open on tiles. He couldn't exactly say 'no'.

"Yes, of course." He wrote the address details on the back of the flyer.

Clinton turned away, and headed out to a room in the back of the shop. Everything was going well with Eliza-May. This was the last thing he needed. He'd have to tell her. They had to find a way to stop James attending. This was their time together. Sick to his stomach, he phoned Appleseeds.

"Hello, Appleseeds. Eliza-May speaking. How may I help you?"

Just hearing her voice calmed him down.

"It's Clinton."

"Hey," she smiled, her face lighting up.

"James is in the shop. He wants to come to the book club. Just thought you should know."

He was taken aback by the silence at the end of the phone.

"Eliza-May?"

If he could see her, Clinton would notice that she was shaking her head in disbelief.

"Do you think he knows about us?" she eventually asked.

He sighed. "I have no idea. I thought we'd been discreet. Eliza-May, if you want to stop this we can. It's not what I want, but I understand if you feel differently now."

"I'm not giving you up, Clinton. I just haven't worked out how to tell James yet. I don't want to stay married to him any longer, but..."

"What is it?"

"He's a strong man. What James wants, James gets. He's not used to people defying him, and he *always* gets his own way. He gave up a lot to follow me here. I need to tread carefully."

"Are you worried he'll hurt you, Eliza-May?"

"No, not like that. Not physically. I can't talk now, there are customers coming into the shop. Umm, you know what, I'm not going to come to the book club tonight. I'm sorry, but I just couldn't bear being in your home with him sitting beside me. It would feel wrong. Are you free tomorrow night? Maybe we could go back to that park and take a walk?"

"Of course. I'd love that. Pick you up at five?" Clinton asked.

"I'll be waiting."

Veranda Talk

Car and Astrid sat side by side on the porch swing, sharing a large woolly blanket, and watched the Sun go down over the valley. Colorado pines nodded in the distance. The Autumn mists, a regular feature this week, shrouded the nearby river: a portent of things to come.

"You seem quite bright, Astrid, despite your illness. It's a joy to watch," Car said, squeezing her daughter's hand tightly.

"I feel excited about watching what Bob's doing at Cottonwood. I wake up each day smiling, and giving thanks. You'd think I was Azaria!" she chuckled. "Seriously though, I feel like I have a purpose, even though Bob and Isaac are the ones doing all the work. I'm always keen to know what he's up to, and just bide my time until Azaria has a spare moment to drive me over there."

"You're the heart behind this project, though, and that's what is making you smile. Where there's hope, there's life. Don't underestimate how much healing that place can bring to you." Car closed her eyes, and breathed in the night air.

"I feel different when I'm there. It's a healing sort of place. I feel it in the air. Something about the cottonwoods lining the river, the beautiful flow of the water, and the way the sunlight falls on those upland pastures, just invigorates me. I'm sure I don't feel as tired at the moment. And I keep thinking about what Azaria said: that there's enough water below to host a public water supply. Ma, that just feels so powerful to me. To be in a place of healing, and all that water. What more could we ask for? Ha, apart from a new name for the place."

"I thought you'd just said it, actually."

Astrid looked at her mother quizzically. "What did I say?"

"Healing Waters."

"Oh my, that's perfect. Perfect!"

"You came up with it, honey. They were your words."

Astrid felt the words slide off her tongue: *Healing Waters Residential Home for Single Mothers.*

"I'm so happy, Ma! So happy!"

"I'm happy for you, sweetheart. This is a good thing you're doing. So many women and children will benefit over the years."

"We're all doing it, not just me. It might have been my idea, but all of you are contributing. I just hope we can find the right person to manage the place. It has to be someone who likes women and babies."

"I have no doubt that the right person will walk straight into the job," Car said softly, "just the right person."

"How can you be so sure, Ma?" She looked at Car's knowing smile. "Azaria hasn't dowsed for it, has she?"

"No. Are you warm enough?" Car asked, changing the subject.

"I will be if you snuggle a bit closer," Astrid said, enjoying the evenings they shared on the veranda, where they'd talk for hours. But now, silence filled the air, a balm over the busy day.

Eventually, Astrid asked, "Do you think I can learn to be a mother? I mean, I have no idea how to be when I meet Victoria."

"The first thing will be to call her Mahina. That'd probably get you off to a good start!"

"Oh," she laughed, "that does take some getting used to. I really wish Starr would get in contact more often and let us know what's happening. It's all a bit too cryptic for my liking. And she's been gone ages."

"If anyone can find your daughter, it's our Starr. That girl is like a dog with a bone when she makes up her mind to do something. Just trust her. But yes, you can learn how to be a mother. You already are one, you just haven't had the day-to-day experience of it."

"I feel like my heart is bone dry, and I don't know how to love her. That sort of stuff doesn't come naturally to me like it does to Azaria."

"She's had forty-odd years to become the mother she is today. Don't compare yourself. I couldn't bear it."

"I can't help it. I mean, look at the way she is with Rubes. You'd think that kid was her own daughter. She loves her to bits, but she's really firm in her boundaries. She knows when to say no, and when to give in. It scares me how intuitive she is. I mean, I know she's a bit of a white witch and all that, but she really scares me. Doesn't anything faze her?" Astrid asked, completely perplexed by her sister.

"Don't be fooled by her calm exterior. Azaria feels things deeply, and each time a problem comes up she challenges herself to go within and find a peaceful place inside so she can discover what she needs to do to deal with the situation, but specifically her reaction to it."

"But that's it, really. She just seems to always know what to do. How does a person get to that place where they can respond to life like that?" Astrid asked.

"With practise!" Car said.

"How will I learn to be a mother, though, presuming Victoria, I mean Mahina, wants to have me in her life? We don't have any history. I haven't given her roots. There's nothing substantial to bond us. I can't help thinking about it, and I'm at a loss. You're one of the wisest women I know. Help me." Her words were soft, but stretched with desperation.

"Do you know that moss doesn't need roots to grow? And it can thrive perfectly well without them," Car said.

"No, I didn't know that. Ma, there are so many things I've left unsaid. I just don't know where to start."

"Tell me something, Astrid. When you imagine meeting Mahina, what is the picture you have in your mind?"

Astrid's face fell. "That's the scary part. I can't see it. I can't actually imagine us meeting and embracing, or worse, her telling me to get lost. I just can't see anything. What if she's not even alive? I couldn't bear that."

Car briefly thought about the conversation between Ruby and Isaac, and wondered if she should ask the resident psychic, or would that be putting too much pressure on those young shoulders?

"How do I change it, Ma? How do I imagine our reunion?"

"Honestly? You really want me to answer that?" Car asked.

Astrid sighed. "Yes, I do."

"You need to love yourself, and more than anything, you need to find a way to forgive yourself. Your body is riddled with regret, and to heal, to *really* heal, you have to let that go. Nobody can do that for you."

"You sound just like Azaria! It's not that simple!" she cried.

"I didn't suggest it was simple, Astrid. Healing from emotional pain is never straightforward."

"I wouldn't even know where to start. You're speaking a foreign language. I'm not like you two. I don't know how to do this."

"Shall we start at the beginning?" Car said, coaxing her daughter into the future.

Behind Car Doors

Debating whether to fly or drive to Nashville, Starr opted to drive. She figured it would give her time to come up with a reason to interview Mahina — one she couldn't refuse — or somehow arrange a meeting. It would take the best part of two full days to drive there, but somehow the thought of that didn't deter her too much.

Absorbing the scenery, Starr savoured every moment of her road trip. From time to time she'd talk to Luna, as if she were sitting in the passenger seat. They talked about the look of the Atlantic ocean, and then, later, the salty pungent smell of the marsh soil along the tidal rivers.

When they stopped for a rest along the roadside, they closed their eyes by the ever-stretching limbs of oak trees. Tree frogs sang into the afternoon air. Starr closed her eyes and thanked Goddess that her sister was there, right beside her, a silent — well, not so silent if truth be told — and unseen passenger.

A small market town had Starr pulling over to buy one of the sweetgrass baskets on display. She could feel the distinct history of the place at that roadside stand, where they were tended by descendants of the first inhabitants: Gullah women. As the Sun slipped away, they dined on corn chowder and okra gumbo, and enjoyed sweet potato pie and fresh peaches for dessert. Later, Starr wrote in her journal, describing the road trip with Luna in great detail.

> I feel closer to Luna than ever, and it is deeply comforting. Here, together on the great open road, we chat like she never left:

As if her passing never was that grenade that ripped our family apart. I am enjoying her company. I think of her fiancé, Patrick, and what his future must look like now without their wedding on the horizon. I can only begin to imagine his heartbreak. And, of course, I keep seeing Tobias in my mind. He's different to all the other men I've known. I'm terrified though, if I'm perfectly honest. There are so many plans and dreams I have for my life. I desperately want to travel and see more of the world, but at what cost? Do I end up leaving him on hold while I follow my heart? It's not fair to ask him to wait. He's doing that already, but that's only because he knows I'll be back in Australia before too long. Luna's death has magnified every single detail of my life. I've never been more present to my daily needs, and at another level life feels pointless. The truth is I am searching. I'm so determined to find answers; to understand the meaning of human existence. And another part of me couldn't care less. I just want to keep eating peaches and not have a care in the world.

Starr fell asleep in her car that night, dreams taking her to far-off lands: Luna married Patrick, and was on the porch swing rocking her baby. In the depth of that lucid dream, Starr knew it couldn't possibly be true — Luna was dead — but she sat down with her sister anyway, and stroked the baby's head. Starr hadn't been this happy since her night in the Outback making love with Tobias.

Book Club

James Megane arrived home at 6pm, surprised to find his wife wasn't there. Maybe she planned to go straight to the book club after work. Showering, he took his time, grateful that he was finally taking a concrete step to connecting with his wife. Closing his eyes, he groaned at the realisation that his marriage was at breaking point. He hadn't recognised anything was wrong until Eliza-May's makeover. Alarm bells went off the moment he saw her, and he knew without question that the fine haircut and boutique clothes weren't to impress him, but another man. James had no idea who had caught her eye, but he intended to find out. Book club was certainly a good place to start. He was prepared to do anything, anything at all, to keep his marriage intact.

Splashing on aftershave, James dressed casually in jeans and long-sleeved t-shirt. He placed the gift-wrapped books on Eliza-May's pillow, and then headed to the car.

Not having read fiction since high school, James was sure he'd be out of place, but what he did have in his favour were years of courtroom drama and taking centre stage. He knew how to play a part, and talk his way out of, or into, anything. Tonight would be no different.

Warmly welcomed at the front door by Jenna and Alice, James followed them inside and gratefully received a mug of coffee, and cookies. Clinton kept in the background, engaging in conversation with one of the older book-club members, until it was time to start.

"We'd like to welcome you to our group. I'm sure many of you will know Mr Megane from around town.

He recently set up a law practice here. Shall we begin? This week we're looking at the archetype of the heroine in fiction, and if she can be true to character."

James wasn't listening. Instead, he was double-checking every face in the room, completely miffed as to why Eliza-May wasn't here. Could she have been lying about being part of a book club? Was that just a cover? It threw James, because if there was one thing he knew about his wife it was that she was an avid book reader, generally getting through a couple of hundred novels a year. Where the hell was she? Why had she lied to him?

It would be rude to leave, he knew that, but he couldn't give a damn about heroines, fiction or in real life. He just wanted to find his wife!

"Would you excuse me, I suddenly don't feel well. I'm so sorry, but I'm going to have to leave," James said; then without waiting for a response, left immediately.

Clinton withheld his smile; inside he was cheering.

Eliza-May opened the gift-wrapped parcel on her pillow, and curiously looked at the books James had chosen for her. He signed each of them, with declarations of lifelong love. All three were good choices, and he'd clearly put a lot of thought into his purchases, but she'd read them years ago. She couldn't decide if he knew her well or didn't know her at all. Sure that James wouldn't be home for a few hours, she took out the latest novel from her drawer and decided to enjoy a long bath.

Soaking in the warm, jasmine-scented bubble-topped water, Eliza-May was surprised to discover that she couldn't concentrate on the book, despite it being the latest release from her all-time favourite author. The only thing her mind wanted to think about was Clinton. His attentiveness and kindness had transformed her days.

With him, she felt loved and valued. Each day, she'd be met by him at the start of work, or they'd meet for lunch upstairs in the bookshop, or take a walk in the evenings. Today was the first time they hadn't spent together. And she didn't like it one bit. The time was nearing when she'd have to make the decision to tell James what they both already knew: their marriage was over. It was impossible for her to live as housemates any longer. It was too soon to move in with Clinton, but she'd already given up the tenancy on the house she'd rented when arriving back in Colorado. Maybe she could bunk in with Bella, Chandra and Callum for a bit. No, a bit too cosy. And as much as she loved them, she wanted her own space. Tomorrow she'd start looking for a home to rent. Again.

Why did I move back in with James? she kept asking herself. The day she left New York had cemented the fact there was nothing of their relationship to salvage. Was the only reason they were together now because of his grand gesture? It was a shock to the whole family that he packed up the only life he knew to relocate to Colorado. But why? Why did he do it? He'd had years to make it right between them. She pondered the fact that they hadn't made love since before her depression had kicked in. Not once, even after he moved to Colorado, had he attempted anything other than a goodnight peck on the cheek. She thought of the way Clinton kissed her, and how each time, her knees wobbled. She couldn't remember ever feeling like that with James, not even at the start of their relationship. Desperate to make love with Clinton, and bring their relationship to a new place, she sighed as she remembered the feel of his hands on the small of her back. He had wanted her as much as she had desired him.

Tomorrow. Tomorrow she'd find a new home. And with that thought firmly in place, she picked up the book and began to read.

At the start of chapter two, Eliza-May was surprised to see James standing at the bathroom door.

"Why didn't you go to your book club?" he demanded, thumping the door frame in anger. He reminded her of a tempestuous toddler who hadn't got his own way.

"I felt like an early night. I'm tired."

"Why didn't you tell me you weren't going tonight?"

"You didn't ask, and frankly, you're never here in the evenings, so whether I'm home or not really isn't something I felt needed discussing."

James stormed to the kitchen, and poured himself another glass of rum. Furious, he waited for Eliza-May to finish her bath. He watched the news, drank some more, and paced back and forward. How much longer was she going to be in that damn bathroom? Despite being hampered by his now blurry vision, he refilled his glass.

Even from within the confines of the en suite, Eliza-May could feel the tension. This was the last place she wanted to be. She'd have to tell him tonight, but her heart felt like dark shards of gravel engraved into fragile skin. She didn't even want to see his face, let alone have to engage in the most important conversation of their lives.

Dressing in flannel pyjamas, Eliza-May crawled into bed, and turned out the light. She'd done so quietly so as not to alert him that she was out of the bath. Heart palpitating, she tried to settle her rapid breathing, but to no avail. The light switched on, drenching the room with reality: it was now or never.

James undressed, and climbed into bed. He knew what his wife needed. His hands reached under her top, and grappled her breasts.

"I'm tired, James. Not tonight."

"It'll wake you up. It's what we both need. It's what our marriage needs. I've been missing all the obvious signs. You need me to take notice of you. Well that's what I'm doing now, damn it. This isn't the time to reject me!" he snapped.

She closed her eyes and tried to pretend it was Clinton touching her, but even though they hadn't yet made love, she knew he would hold her in a completely different way.

Rum riddled the air, and she turned her face away from James.

"Look at me Eliza-May. Look in my eyes while I make love to you," his words slurred one after the other.

The last thing she felt was love. Nor like. And definitely not lust.

"You're my wife!" he growled.

She did as instructed and looked into his eyes. All she could see was a wounded boy. Part of her felt sorry for him. James had spent his life as a high achiever, desperate to make a mark in the legal world. His father was a high-court judge, and nothing James ever did felt like it was good enough. But was this Eliza-May's problem? Hadn't she supported him for years on end? It was time to look after herself.

"I...I don't want you to make love to me," she croaked, as his hand slid inside her underwear, seeking out her dampness.

Dry. She was drier than the desert. Pulling down her pyjama bottoms and ripping off her panties, James spat onto his hand and used the saliva to lubricate her.

"This will help," he muttered.

"No, James. Don't. Don't do this! I don't want it!" With all the courage she could muster, she blurted it out: "I don't love you anymore, James."

"You've just forgotten how good we are together.

It's been too long. You're out of practice, but you'll warm up in a minute. It's just like riding a bicycle. You don't ever forget." His words made her feel ill.

"I said 'no'. Get off me!"

As he entered her, his eyes closed at the pleasure of her tightness around him, James was oblivious to the tears settling, like stagnant ponds, upon her cheeks. Afterwards, the rum finally got the better of him and he slumped over her, exhausted, drunk, snoring.

Silent tears turned to sobs. Unable to move him off her, Eliza-May eventually fell asleep with her head against the sopping-wet pillow.

Tomorrow, that was her mantra: *Tomorrow was a new day.*

Music In Her Blood

Butterflies on double-shot espresso buzzed through her belly, leaving Starr on the verge of throwing up. She'd never experienced such nervousness in her life. Letting the rental car idle, she stayed at the bottom of the poplar-tree-lined driveway for some time, plotting her next move. Should she just turn up at Mahina's house and say 'hey there, I'm your long lost cousin', or would it be better, perhaps, to seek out an interview and get to know her through a different lens? No matter which way she turned it, Starr couldn't decide. There was no easy way to handle this. Even if Mahina hadn't been a world-famous country-music artist, the matter was still delicate.

Turning off the car's engine, Starr pulled a sandwich out of her backpack. *If the roles were reversed,* she wondered, *how would I want to find out that I had a family somewhere?* Putting herself in someone else's shoes was something Starr did regularly in her line of work, to help her maintain an objective view. But how could she possibly ask the question of herself, given that her only experience of family life was one that had provided her with such strong roots, endless lengths of love which reached into the depths of her being, and set her on a path in life where she felt as if she could fly? She had no idea how to break the news. What would her mother suggest? She didn't want to tell Azaria just yet who Victoria really was, in case Astrid decided to make contact directly. This was a situation that needed handling with care, and if there was anything Starr knew about her aunty it was that she was impulsive. Cancer, of course, had changed Astrid a lot, but Starr wasn't taking any chances.

Maybe she should confide in Bob or Car? An old

memory surfaced in Starr's mind. She was seven years old, and had a friend visiting. Some money had been stolen from a jar on the kitchen bench. Starr knew that neither she nor Luna had pinched it, so the only other person could be Nigella. There was no way that her friend was going to admit to it, and eventually Starr confessed that she'd taken it. Azaria, of course, knew that although Starr was a minx and the family's trickster, she wasn't a thief.

Later on, Azaria had said "I know you didn't take the money and were protecting your friend, which is honourable, but it's not honest. Honesty is always the best policy. I thought I'd taught you that? The quicker we tell the truth, no matter how painful it might be for everyone involved, the sooner we can all find peace. Nigella now thinks she has gotten away with her little crime, and that means she might try it next time she visits."

"I've decided that I don't want to have her here again." Starr had crossed her arms defiantly. "I don't want her here!" she'd cried, storming off to her treehouse behind the barn.

Was this memory a message? A voice telling her to be direct with Mahina? She sighed. Turning the key in the ignition, Starr closed her eyes and whispered "Help me do this, Luna. Wherever you are, help me tell our cousin who she really is. Please." And as if a load was suddenly taken off her shoulders, she inched the car along the driveway until she arrived at Fort Knox. At least that's what it felt like. Of course Mahina would have security! It was public knowledge that she valued her privacy above all else. Damn. *Damn!*

She pressed a button at the gate, and when a man's voice asked who was there, Starr simply replied "I'm Starr Linden."

"Do you have an appointment with Miss Safiya. I

can't see your name on our register."

"No," she said honestly, knowing she could have cited a media interview, "I don't have an appointment. I'm Mahina's cousin."

"Just one moment please."

One moment stretched out like an eternity before morphing into five minutes and 23 seconds.

"I'm sorry, your entry has been denied. Miss Safiya does not have any cousins."

There was nothing for it. It killed Starr to be so blunt, but it was now or never. She'd come too far to be turned away. "I'm her biological cousin."

"I'm sorry?"

"I'm the niece of her birth mother. She will know what you mean."

The voice of the security guard went quiet, and it was almost 85 minutes before he returned, his voice soft through the speaker.

"Please drive through, Starr Linden. Miss Safiya will see you now."

Oh my God! Starr whispered. She was in! She was actually being allowed in. Her hands were shaking, and it was all she could do to keep them steady on the steering wheel. Simultaneously laughing and crying, she wanted to call her family right away and tell them the fabulous news. But, she'd wait. She'd wait until she'd actually met her cousin, and then report back. "Oh my God!" she squealed.

The driveway continued for another 300 yards, sliding to the left, beyond a forest of red cedar trees, and then, like a tableau, the most incredible house appeared before Starr.

"Whoah, no wonder she wants her privacy. Man, I wouldn't share this place either. Jeez!"

Nestled against an imposing mountainside, the

majestic home fitted perfectly into the surrounding landscape: the autumnal leaves of mustard, claret and rust made a spectacular display.

Starr breathed in deeply, and headed up the wide stone staircase to the large glass front door. The entire house frontage comprised of floor-to-ceiling windows. Starr turned around to face the view. *Amazing,* she whispered. *Amazing.*

Timidly tapping the door, she was greeted by the man who had answered the security system. He looked her up and down, with curiosity more than anything.

"Miss Safiya will be down shortly. Come through here, and make yourself comfortable. My name is Carnell. If there's anything you need, just ring," he said, motioning to a small brass bell on the table. Beside it was a tray of food, and he began to pour her a drink. "Miss Safiya thought you might like to join her for brunch. But help yourself, don't wait for her. She could be a few minutes, yet."

Starr found herself unable to speak. Her cousin actually wanted to eat with her? Mahina was trusting that they were cousins without even double-checking? It surprised Starr. She had expected to be interrogated to within an inch of her life.

"Thank you," she said, mindful that Carnell was obviously in shock too.

He nodded graciously, then left the room. With rumbling tummy, her mouth watered when examining the choices before her: waffles and maple syrup, eggs Benedict, hash browns, jalapeño and Cheddar balls. There was a cafetière of hot coffee. She contemplated whether it would jolt her nervous system anymore than it already had been, and chose freshly squeezed grapefruit juice instead. *Oh how the other half live,* she mused, despite coming from a priviledged background herself.

It was like something out of a fairytale, that moment…that moment when Starr first set eyes on the person whose absence in the family had made her larger than life itself. Descending the wide, curved staircase, Mahina entered the spacious downstairs room as elegantly as if she were accepting an award. Her turquoise dress floated behind her, the fabric unsure it should be going down the stairs.

With spicy jalapeño in her mouth, Starr gobbled the last piece down and wiped her fingers across her faded denim jeans. Of all the days to be underdressed!

"Hi," Starr said softly, struck that Mahina's beauty was quite mesmeric. Without a trace of make-up, she looked somewhat different to all the photos in glossy magazines. The family resemblance was immediate, and Starr couldn't believe that over all the years of being such a huge fan she'd never made the connection.

"I'm Starr."

"We're cousins, then, huh?" Mahina shook Starr's hand, and then sat down and poured herself coffee.

"Yes, we are."

"My best friend doesn't even know I was adopted, so I can't for the life of me figure out how you would know. You're not a journalist, are you?"

"Well, first and foremost, I'm most definitely your cousin. Your birth mother, Astrid, is my Mom's twin sister. I am a journalist, as it happens, but your secret is safe with me. I'm not here to write a story or expose you in any way. You have my word on that."

"I'm supposed to trust someone I've never met?" she said suspiciously.

"I'm family."

"So?" Mahina shrugged her shoulders.

"Well, in my family, that word is sacred. If we offer our word, we mean it."

"I don't know anything about your family, sweetie."

"I'm your family. I hope you'll learn to trust me."

"Why are you here? That part of my life was a long time ago. I really don't need to dredge up any memories." She let out a sarcastic laugh. "Not that I have any memories! I have my life just the way I like it. There's no need for me to include so-called family. My friends are my family."

Where to from here? It was one thing being allowed in the door, but Mahina wasn't giving an inch.

In a flash, Starr remembered her mother's words: *if you want someone to trust you, you have to share a piece of your soul.*

"Last Christmas, my life changed forever. You see, our mothers are twins, but I'm a twin, too. The thing is, my identical twin sister, Luna, was killed in an earthquake."

Mahina's face visibly changed to one of distress.

"She did?"

"It tore our family apart. I see life so differently now. Mostly, I don't want to waste a single day. I don't want regrets, and I want to do good where I can."

"I'm sincerely sorry about Luna. I don't have any siblings, but I do know loss. It must be breaking your hearts. I'm so sorry."

"We'll never recover, that's for sure. In our own ways, we're absorbing the pain. Each day is a new start, but it's also another day without her."

"Yes, death is tough on those left behind. Starr, how did you find me? It can't have been easy."

"You're right! Well, my grandmother, Car," Starr's face lit up. "She's 81 and plays the guitar and drums. You'd love her!"

Despite her passion, she saw the walls go up and Mahina's poker face come into play. Clearly the woman didn't want to be drawn into this unknown family.

"Anyway, Granny Car had a photo of you from the day you were born."

"Really, there's a photo of me as a baby?" The idea seemed too unreal.

Starr said "Here, I'll show you." She rifled about in her backpack, until she found the small notebook which held the photocopy she'd taken.

Mahina looked at the photo for several minutes, not saying a word.

"Go on," she instructed.

"Well, I had the photo and I knew where you'd been born, so I asked Astrid for details about your birth."

"My birth mother's dead, though."

"Astrid? No. No, she's alive. Your biological father, sadly, is dead."

Mahina let out a long sigh.

"I grew up believing both my parents were dead. She's alive, and she never came to look for me?" There was anger in Mahina's voice now. "She let me go! She let her baby go? What sort of woman does that?"

"You need to understand…"

"Understand what? That she didn't want me?"

"It really wasn't that simple. Will you please let me explain?" Starr pleaded.

"Don't make some lame excuse that she was a busy career woman and didn't have time, because I really couldn't stomach that."

"Your mother was 16 years old, and estranged from her family. She had no way of raising a baby on her own."

"Where the hell was my father, then? Why couldn't he or his family take me in?"

"Mahina, your father was a firefighter. His name was Rory. He and your Mom were madly in love. They'd actually run away to be together. You have to know that despite them being young, you were created by two people who loved each other."

"So where was he?" Mahina demanded.

"Just before you were born, Rory was killed in a fire."

Mahina gasped. "No. No. That can't be."

"I'm so sorry. He died trying to save a baby inside a blazing inferno. The tragedy was that he never got to meet his own baby. If he'd survived, your mother would never have given you up. Of that, I'm certain. She was alone in a strange place, widowed, traumatised, and then went into labour with you. She wasn't thinking straight."

Mahina stood up and paced the room, before standing at the front windows looking at the sweeping views before her. For four decades she'd believed that her parents had died.

"Does my mother know you're here? That you've found me?"

"Astrid was desperate for me to find you, and she knows I'm on your trail, but she doesn't know who you are, or where I am. Mahina, I'm sorry that I came here unannounced and landed on your doorstep with all this information. If there'd been an easier way to tell you, please know that I would have."

"If she was so desperate, then why isn't she here? Doesn't sound desperate to me that she sent you instead. Sounds cowardly. Really cowardly."

"Astrid's life hasn't been easy."

"*Her* life hasn't been easy? She got off scott free without a baby she brought into this world."

"A baby she had every intention of keeping if you'd arrived in the circumstances in which she expected you to be born."

"It's not my fault that my father died!"

"I wasn't remotely suggesting it was. Mahina, I know you're upset and it's a lot to take in. Astrid's not here because…she's dying. She's got cancer. Travel's not an option right now."

Mahina turned away from Starr and looked out the windows again.

"So, she's not really desperate to meet her long-lost daughter, is she? What she is really after is my forgiveness. It's a classic end-of-life-regret thing she's got going on. Tell her she can die in peace. I won't hold it against her. Are we done here?" Mahina faced Starr, looking her firmly in the eye.

"I want to get to know you," Starr said with a depth of sincerity that brought tears to her eyes.

"I deal with groupies every day, I really don't need anymore."

"I want to get to know you as my cousin. I have every album you ever made, and probably every press cutting. I've been a fan for years. There's nothing you can tell me about your professional life that I don't already know. You, Mahina. I want to know you. You're my family. For all my childhood you were like a ghost figure: there, but not there. We said prayers for you every goddamn night! Please don't dismiss me like I'm no one. I am your family, and you are mine." Starr was desperate now.

"Why on Earth would you say prayers for me?" Mahina was taken aback by the revelation.

"We grew up loving you. Not a day went by when your name wasn't mentioned. Though, of course, we knew you as Victoria."

Mahina shook her head.

Carnell entered the room, and asked "Is there anything else you need, Miss?"

"Yes, can you check that the guest room on the left

wing is made up ready for my cousin? She will be staying with me for a while."

"Yes, I'll see that it's sorted right away."

"Thank you. We're going for a walk. We'll eat lunch in the conservatory in a couple of hours. Would you make us those delightful barbecue beans and spicy cornbread?"

"Yes, of course," he replied, looking at Starr and wondering what to make of her.

"Follow me," Mahina said to Starr. "I'll get you some walking shoes. Same size as me by the look of it."

They walked in silence for some time, Starr taking in the stunning scenery. Sunlight filtered through the trees as they trekked beneath a canopy of yellow poplars.

"You live in a beautiful place."

"I do. I've always lived in beautiful places. I've been lucky that way," reflected Mahina.

"I...went to the lighthouse," Starr confessed.

"You did?"

"It's closed."

"I know."

"Have you been there recently?"

"I bought it a few years back when I discovered the government had put it up for sale. It never occurred to me that it didn't belong to my parents. I'm not sure what I'll do with it. Haven't got the heart to go through all our things. It's not a shrine, as such, but it feels like something I want to keep just for me, if you know what I mean?"

"Mahina," Starr said, slowing down to a stop and putting her hand on her cousin's shoulder. "I was devastated to hear what happened to Bernice and Steven. I'm so sorry."

"It was life-changing. There were good things

to come out of it...all this...I wouldn't have moved to Nashville and created my dream career if they'd stayed alive...but God they were good to me. The best parents you could imagine! I mean, they were busy people, and it must have been so hard to have a moody 12-year-old thrust into their care, but they fed me well, bought me books, talked to me long into the night about whatever I wanted to know. They listened to me painstakingly teach myself guitar. Not a pretty sound! More than anything, they were kind. Ever so kind and patient. I miss them, ya know?"

"Yeah, I do. My dad died a long time ago, but I still miss him. It's hard losing a parent, really hard."

"And now you've lost a sister too? That sucks!"

"But I've gained a cousin," Starr smiled.

"I think you might have, yes. Tell me more about your family. Do you have any other family members?"

"Sure. There's Mom, of course. She's a bit woo-woo, but everyone loves her despite the incense, meditation and divination she does using beeswax."

Mahina raised her eyebrows. "She sounds *interesting*."

"She's one of a kind. What makes me laugh is how different Astrid is...I mean, they are chalk and cheese. Astrid considers all that stuff absolute nonsense. There's also Granny Car. I reckon that's where you get your music from. I have two older sisters. Kara is only a little younger than you. She's volunteering at an orphanage in Zululand."

"That's amazing," Mahina said.

"Yeah, she's pretty dedicated to humanitarian issues. She doesn't have kids of her own. There's Eliza-May, who is married to James, an attorney." Her heart sank at the thought of their marriage, and the possible fallout. "She has two daughters. Not twins!"

Starr laughed. "Bella has a baby of her own now. Little Chandra is only a few months old, and so adorable. Ruby is in high school. In some ways, she's a mini-Azaria. And our family has some really cool men in it, now. Mom has a lovely beau, Isaac. I reckon they'll get married one day. If he can pin her down with a suitable date. They're always in each other's pockets. And Astrid is married to Bob. Bob's real nice. So good for her."

"So she found love at last?" Mahina said, bitterness at the edge of her words.

"Eventually! But that's a whole other story."

"I've got time. I'd like to hear it," Mahina said, smiling, her face losing its early guarded expression.

Mirror Mirror On The Wall

"I feel stupid," Astrid said, sitting before Car's oval mirror.

"That feeling will pass. Trust me. Try it again," Car suggested kindly.

"I love you, Astrid." Astrid whispered to her image in the mirror. "Ma, it's dumb. This isn't going to transform me into a mother!"

"Honey, I know you're sceptical of anything and everything, but you asked for my help, and this is our starting point." Car held her hands on Astrid's shoulders, smiling at her face in the mirror and bending down to kiss her scalp. "Come on, try it again," she coaxed gently.

Astrid raised her eyebrows.

"Tell me something, Astrid. When Bob tells you he loves you, does that feel stupid?"

"Of course not!"

"If he can love you, and I love you, then surely that must tell you that you're loveable."

Astrid sighed, looking at the worn hands resting in her lap. "But it's different. You're my mother, you have to love me."

"No I don't. Not at all. I *choose* to love you. I have always chosen to love you. Okay, let's try this: How about telling yourself that you are ready to forgive yourself?"

"Crap. Honestly, Ma, you're not making this easy for me."

"When did I ever say this was easy? You want to heal. You want to feel motherhood in your heart. So, the starting point has to be in recognising who you are, and loving yourself no matter what."

Car looked into her daughter's eyes. "Astrid, I love

you. Sweetheart, I forgive you. Astrid," she said, a tear escaping from her left eye, "I *see* you."

Astrid felt every word ripple through her body, and into a place that time forgot. Unconditional love moved her to tears.

"I...don't feel worthy of your love. I've let you down so many times, Ma."

"What you think of as failure, I see as choices and lessons upon your life path. How can any of that be wrong?" Car asked tenderly.

"When you put it like that..."

Astrid's view returned to her reflection in the mirror.

"Hey," she gasped. "Is that hair growing back?"

Car laughed. "You've only just noticed?"

"Oh my goodness. What does that mean? Am I... am I healing?"

"Who knows? But it's certainly put a skip in my step."

Astrid cried gently for a few moments, relieved, shocked, hopeful. It seemed impossible. Slowly, her gaze returned to the bald woman staring at her in the mirror. A woman whose body had been ravaged by cancer. A woman whose body had borne a daughter, and spent four decades silently grieving. A woman who had turned her life around, and was learning to help other people. A woman who, despite having experienced death and pain in relationships, had learnt to love again.

No longer did she see a weak and pathetic person in front of her, but someone who had walked a trial by fire, and reached a point of power. She'd chosen to find her daughter. She had chosen to be a wounded healer, and build a residential home for single mothers. And now, here, with her mother as a guide, she would choose to love herself.

"I've been through a lot in my life, haven't I?" Astrid asked, hoping for reassurance.

"Indeed. And look at how far you've come, and what you've achieved. It's incredible. You are incredible. I'm so proud of you, Astrid. I'm proud to call you my daughter."

Astrid's face screwed up at the impossibility of her mother loving her no matter what, and she fought the urge to cry.

"Damn it, Astrid, I love you!" Astrid yelled at her reflection. "You are a strong and powerful woman. I forgive you. I forgive you for running away from home. I forgive you for hurting your family. I forgive you for giving your baby away. I forgive you for closing your heart to love and life." She stopped there, her face radish red, and tears streaming down her face. Her ears burned crimson.

"Don't stop now, honey, you're on a roll," Car smiled, making herself comfortable on the bed.

Calming her breath down, and regaining some composure, Astrid looked into her mother's eyes. "I'm sorry I rejected you so many times, just because your beliefs about life were different to mine. I'm sorry I felt so embarrassed by you in front of my school friends, with your dreadlocks and hippy clothes. Everyone referred to you as the white witch on the hill. It used to upset me so much. They weren't unkind, ever, but it always made me feel different to everyone else. I hated it. For a time, I hated you. I hated our hippy life here on the mountaintop. Please forgive me, Ma. If I could go back in time I would do everything differently. Everything! Who knows, maybe I would even have embraced all this."

"It is what it is, my love. There are no mistakes."

"Do you really believe that?" Astrid asked in disbelief, angry that what had been a huge issue in her life was just a dot to Car.

"Yes I do." Car embraced her daughter and said "Must be time for a cup of tea. I'll put the kettle on. Licorice tea?"

Astrid nodded, but stayed in the room. Once Car closed the door behind her, Astrid looked in the mirror again.

"I love you. I'm sorry. Please forgive me. Thank you." She breathed out deeply. Something felt different. She wasn't sure what. Maybe it was just because she'd had a good cry.

Homecoming

Isaac counted down the minutes till Martin arrived. They were meeting at Appleseeds, and then they'd head to Isaac's house. Eliza-May made Isaac a coffee. She could tell he was excited, and probably needed a chamomile tea instead, but since she was making herself one, decided to pour two cups.

"How long has it been since you've seen your son and grandkids?"

"Years! Not since he left Honduras." Somehow he regretted saying the name, as it would forever more be associated with Luna's death.

"How long are they staying?"

"Not sure. A week or so I guess. He'll need to get back for the new academic term. I'm surprised they're coming at all, but I'm grateful."

"I look forward to meeting them. But, for now, Isaac, make yourself useful and go and sit down over there with your drink. You're driving me crazy with your pacing. Oh, you know what, I think I've got some of those lovely honey and almond cookies out the back. I'll get you some." She disappeared behind a curtain and returned with a plate. "I've got work to do," she said sternly, hoping it would keep him seated.

For several minutes she added new stock to the shelves: an assortment of fruit teas, cruelty-free make-up, plant-based soaps, and packets of seeds and nuts. When the doorbells tinkled, she turned around to see if it was Martin.

"Kara? Kara! I didn't know you were coming back! Does Mom know? Come here! Give me a hug!" Eliza-May demanded. They laughed, they cried, and they slow-hugged.

Isaac came over and joined them. "Your Mom said you were thinking of coming back. She'll be thrilled to know you're here."

"I never thought I'd come back, but one day it hit me: I want my family around me…so, here I am. I just need to find a job pretty quickly," Kara added.

"Why didn't you go straight home?" Eliza-May asked.

"I didn't want to arrive empty handed. I know there are lot of mouths to feed at the homestead these days, what with Bob and Astrid and Ruby."

"And me!" Isaac laughed. "I'll get you a basket. Take anything you want from here. Not that Azaria's pantry is empty."

"It's never empty!" Kara and Eliza-May said at the same time.

"I can't believe how good it is to be here. Everything is so comfortable and familiar. I love it!"

"Hey, before you head up the hill, do you want to meet Chandra?" Eliza-May asked her.

"Of course!"

"Bella usually comes by about this time of day. Hang around for a bit."

"My son and grandkids are arriving here any minute; actually I thought they'd be here by now. I'd love you to stick around and say hello. They won't be in town for long."

"Sure, that'd be great."

"Coffee?" Eliza-May asked.

"Never thought you'd ask," Kara said, giving her sister another hug.

When Martin walked through the door, his head nearly scraping the top of the doorway, Kara recognised the resemblance straight away. The sculpted jaw line and

151

amber eyes were a giveaway.

"Martin!" Isaac yelled, delighted. "You're here!" They embraced, their bear-like hugs cementing what was obviously an unbreakable bond. When they pulled apart, Isaac asked "Where are the boys?" He put his head around the front door, looking down the street.

"They're not here, they're off doing their own thing."

"You didn't bring them?" Isaac asked, perplexed.

"Long story, Dad. Mind if I tell you later? I'm pooped, and could do with a rest."

"Of course. Let me introduce you to Azaria's daughters. This is Eliza-May, she runs this place."

"I've heard plenty about you," Martin said, shaking her hand. "Sounds like you're everything Dad needs for keeping this shop running smoothly."

"Thank you. It's a great job. I love it, and am very grateful for being given the chance to manage Appleseeds."

"And this is Kara, who coincidentally has just walked in the door from a long-haul flight too," Isaac said, introducing them.

When their eyes met, Kara knew what had drawn her home. Across time and space, she had felt him calling her. For weeks she'd been dreaming of a man...he was saying her name each night as she slept: 'come home now'. She thought it was just a message to see her mother, but now she knew. Her words came out all jumbled.

He wasn't any more articulate.

Eliza-May and Isaac looked at each other, then she said "You know, I think these two need a coffee. Isaac, take them over there to sit down and we'll get some food into them. Isaac?"

"Yes, yes, of course. Martin, Kara, come over here and make yourselves comfortable."

The chemistry between them knocked Eliza-May sideways. It was the last thing she expected, and was grateful for the pleasant distraction from the rumblings of discontent in her own life.

Serving a few customers first, Eliza-May joined them for a quick coffee. "I'm so glad to have you home sis, I could really do with a girly chat when you've caught up on sleep."

"No worries. Anytime." She smiled at her younger sister, glad to be home.

"Seems silly for us to go in different directions," Isaac said. "Why don't we all head up to Azaria's and make an evening of it? You want to join us Eliza-May, or do you have plans?"

"I'd love to," she said, grasping an escape route from an evening with James. He was unlikely to work late, and although she was desperate to be with Clinton, this family gathering would provide a legitimate reason not to be home.

"Aunty Kara!" Bella called, as she entered the shop. "No one told me you were coming home!"

She passed Chandra to Eliza-May and swooped in for a big hug.

"Surprise! Now, show me that beautiful baby." Kara's heart ached. She'd do anything to have her own baby, but was reconciled to it not being her destiny. "She's got your nose, Bella. And your ears. You both look so well."

"I have a great team of helpers, and you should see my flat upstairs. It's awesome. Gran made it all Bohemian themed. So cool."

Kara laughed. Despite Bella now having the responsibilities of motherhood, she didn't seem that much different than any other teen.

"Would you like to cuddle her?" Bella asked. She

passed the baby over, before waiting for her aunty to reply.

"Oh yes, I'd like that very much." Kara snuggled into the baby's neck, breathing in her delicious scent. Oh what she'd do to have a baby of her own.

Chandra was loved and cuddled and rocked for a full hour until the only person that was needed was Bella. Feed time. Isaac asked if she fancied coming to Azaria's for dinner.

"Sure, we'll come up as soon as Callum's finished work. Can we bring anything?"

"Don't worry about that. We can all pitch in and help when we get there. Shall we lock up now Eliza-May?"

"Yes, of course. She closed down the till, and did some end-of-the day jobs. Just as they were filing out the door, Clinton came along.

"Hey Clinton," Isaac said, playfully slapping him on the back. "Keeping well?"

"Great. Thanks. And you?"

"Top of the world. Ah, Eliza-May's just closing up now. Is there something you needed?" Isaac asked, keen to help.

"Ah, no, nothing that can't wait," he smiled, taking in Eliza-May's beauty, desperate to hold her in his arms.

She answered his thoughts: "We're all going up to my Mom's for dinner. This is my sister Kara, and Isaac's son, Martin. A bit of a family reunion. I guess I'll see you tomorrow morning for your usual?" she said, savouring every second of eye contact.

"Indeed."

They smiled at each other, holding their secret deep within. How far away tomorrow seemed.

Azaria kept interrupting her vegetable chopping to hug

Kara. Within minutes of their arrival, Car and Azaria had sensed something between Martin and Kara. Despite the chaos in the kitchen, everyone assigned to a different job, and baby Chandra demanding to be cuddled by whoever was closest, the meal ended up being created, and delicious aromas mingled in the kitchen. Azaria couldn't have been happier. Her home was vibrating with love, and the laughter filling this room was like a sacred ointment on recent wounds. She gathered everyone around the table to eat.

"How long are you here for?" Car asked Martin.

He looked at Isaac. He hadn't had a chance to tell him yet. There was nothing for it. He may as well find out now.

"I applied for a job nearby."

Isaac laughed out loud. "You're a marine biologist. We're nowhere near the sea here, son."

"It's an environmental-conservation project, actually. Twenty-minutes drive from here. Not great paying, but it's what I need right now."

"Is everything okay? Your boys okay?"

"Yeah, they're just fine, Dad. I need a change, that's all. And I figured it would be nice to be near you again. We used to have so much fun. I miss that."

Azaria felt a lump form in her throat. She knew it would mean the world to Isaac. She'd witnessed, day after day, how amazing he'd been with her family, and now she'd get to see him with his son.

"Well, I for one am glad you're here. And you, too, Kara. It's great to have you home," Isaac said, his hand resting gently on his son's shoulder.

Bob asked, "So Kara, your Mom mentioned you're looking for a job." His mind was working overtime. But before she had a chance to answer, Bob could see Car grinning from ear to ear. "Okay, Car, what is it that's tickled your funny bone?"

She shook her head from side to side.

Kara tied her hair up into a ponytail, then said "I'm keen to do something which makes a difference. I've got lots of skills in humanitarian work and social causes. Not likely that there's that much of that type of thing in the immediate area. I might have to head over to Denver."

Azaria invited everyone to bow their heads in gratitude, and led them in prayer.

Thank you for the food before us
Thank you for the family beside us
Thank you for the love within us
Amen

Bob waited until the meal was served, before sharing the job vacancy at Healing Waters.

"You'd be perfect for it, Kara," Bob insisted.

"I'm in the country how many hours and a job lands in my lap?" she laughed.

"Divine timing," whispered Car.

"Right place, right time," Azaria said, laughing. "It's the law of attraction. When we desire something, the Universe shifts to make it happen."

"Looks like we're both settling down," Martin said, smiling at Kara. He'd hardly taken his eyes off her the whole evening.

"Amazing," she said to Bob whilst looking at Martin. "When would I start?"

Woodsmoke

The first telltale sign that Fall had truly arrived on the mountain was always the lingering hint of woodsmoke on the crisp evening air. Astrid felt the marking of time stamp its way into her life, and thought about how each year her mother and sister would step into this season with a sense of the days becoming darker, and the need to embrace the inevitable 'going within'. They'd collect their Autumnal harvest of pumpkins, squash, blueberries; and bottle preserves for the Winter.

Astrid was resigned to the fact that it was probably the last time she'd experience the majestic Autumn leaves. She sat at the window of the loft, gentle jazz music in the background, and surveyed the land outside. This stunning property had been her childhood home, but the eyes with which she saw it now were completely different. No wonder Azaria had never wanted to leave. Everything about this place was beautiful. The golden aspen leaves dominated the landscape, but a garland of dark-green pines, and pockets of mustard and maroon leaves also had their say.

In the distance, she could see Azaria and Isaac, hand in hand, walking through the orchard. Fog was pushing its way into the late afternoon, but they strolled along like young lovers as if they had all the time in the world. Astrid wondered how she and her sister had ever managed to share the same womb: chalk and cheese.

She couldn't help but smile when Isaac stopped and pulled Azaria into his arms, slowing her down with a soft kiss. Astrid's thoughts were interrupted by Bob arriving with a cup of chamomile tea.

"Here, love. Tea. Anything else I can get you? I'm

just running you a bath."

Astrid pointed out the window. "She makes life look so easy, doesn't she?"

Bob smiled. "They're a great couple. But so are we, Astrid. You and I are a terrific team. It's just that you're looking out there, instead of in here. Look around you. We're living in a beautiful space, thanks to the kindness of that woman out the window."

Astrid looked around the barn conversion. The air was inevitably infused with the scent of beeswax and honey from the barn downstairs. The wood and stone building featured large windows with views that went for miles. The open-plan living area had been tastefully decorated with large indoor plants, colourful cushions, and the expansive wooden floorboards featured handmade rugs.

"I am blessed. I know that. It's just that no matter what life throws at Azaria, she just seems to gracefully glide through those traumas. With me, any little disturbance just eats away at me. I get irritated and angry so quickly. She just seems to be a walking peace flag!"

"Don't compare yourself to her. Maybe let her inspire you, but don't focus on what she has. Look at all that is good in your life and celebrate that."

"My God, *Bob*, you're even starting to sound like my sister!" Astrid laughed.

Bob sat on the sofa and said: "You're the best thing that's ever happened in my life, Astrid. I want to enjoy every day that we have together, and those days will be even more special if you could focus on them too."

"Message received loud and clear."

She eased her way onto the sofa beside Bob, and snuggled into his arms. Safe. That's how she felt. Always safe and protected.

Justice or Revenge?

Family meeting 6pm. Our house. It's urgent.

Eliza-May read through the text from James, and inwardly groaned. She'd planned to meet Clinton at Ploughman's Park.

Bella entered Appleseeds and said "Just had a weird text from Dad about some urgent family meeting. What's going on?"

"I have no idea," Eliza-May sighed.

"Are you and Dad okay?" Bella asked, jiggling Chandra on her hip.

"Honestly? We haven't been okay for years. Probably since just after Rubes was born."

"What happened?"

"Looking back, my depression was probably triggered by the mild postpartum depression. I just wanted to be in the countryside and not stuck up in a high-rise apartment."

"But that was long ago, and you're still together."

"We live under the same roof. That's it. We're not together." Eliza-May tugged at her hem.

"You mean you don't have sex?" Bella asked bluntly.

Eliza-May blushed, and then remembering the events of the other night felt her stomach turn. "It's not about sex. It's about everything. I feel invisible to your Dad. I have for a long time."

"I thought he bought you flowers the other week?" Bella said, exasperated.

"One bouquet of flowers does not a marriage make," Eliza said firmly.

"If this is about you and Dad, then why do I have to

go to this dumb meeting? I've got my own life now. I'm not a kid anymore. Jeez, Chandra's proof of that!"

"I don't know the answer, sweetie. But, for everyone's sake, do you think you could be there? Without Callum?"

"Sure, but I'm not staying for long."

"Hey, we had these new almond cookies come today. They're marketing samples. Do you want to try some?"

"Sure!" Bella said eagerly.

Bella stayed in the health store for a while, occasionally helping out with customers and stocking shelves. Sensing her mother could do with the company, she kept finding jobs to do.

At the close of business, she said "I'm just going to go upstairs to meet Callum when he comes in from work. See you at 6pm," she raised her eyebrows as if in surrender.

"See you then." Eliza-May smiled at her daughter, thankful for her support.

Watching her head back upstairs to her flat, Eliza-May waited impatiently by the front door to see if Clinton had received her text. And there, there he was, walking quickly up the street towards Appleseeds. She smiled to see that he wasn't prepared to let another day go by. He stepped inside the health store, and Eliza-May put up the 'closed' sign, and held his hand as they walked out to a back room.

"I'm so sorry," she whispered. "He said something about a family meeting. Given the state he's been in lately, I don't feel it would be right to let the girls go and not turn up."

"I understand. I'd hoped we could be together properly by now, but I will wait for as long as it takes. Sort your family out, and do what needs to be done. I'll be here, waiting. I promise."

He didn't wait for her reply, but simply kissed her. Her open mouth yielded to him, and the built-up tensions of recent days threatened to leave them both stranded on the storeroom floor.

"Not yet," he groaned. "When we make love, I want you to be somewhere comfortable. You're better than this. I know this room is all we have right now, but I am prepared to wait."

"It's killing me. I've never known such torture." She kissed his unshaven cheek.

"Eliza-May, we have the rest of our lives. We will make every day count, I know we will. I treasure you. I love you."

It was all she could do but cry against his strong shoulders.

"I don't know why you love me, but it has changed my life. It's changed me, and I never want to go back to the person I was."

"You never will. You are far stronger than you know. Somehow you'll find a way to use that strength to make the changes you need."

"I'm glad you have faith in me."

Ruby phoned Azaria. "Gran, I'm in town so won't be back in time for dinner. Can you save me some?"

"Sure, what's going on?" Azaria asked, surprised by the sudden notice.

"Dad's called an emergency family meeting. I've no idea what's going on. Can you pick me up when it's done? I'm sorry to be a nuisance."

"Of course. Just let me know when. Love you, Rubes."

"Love you more, Gran."

Ending the call, Ruby picked up her school bag and wandered along the main street of town. She had another half an hour till she had to be at her father's house, and was determined not to get there a minute too soon. Ruby rather enjoyed window shopping, and imagined buying several dresses, and half a bushel of oranges. When she stopped outside A Novel Idea, her eyes caught two books that she would most definitely buy when she'd earnt the money. Luna was there, her voice always close these days, saying "It's him."

"Huh?" Ruby replied out loud, not caring if anyone thought she was talking to herself.

"Your Mom's new man."

She dismissed the message, and thought it was her imagination. Perhaps she'd spent too many of her study breaks in the bookshop, and had romanticised the notion of her mother being with another book lover.

Feeling unsettled, Ruby continued to walk. Her legs, heavy now, reluctantly headed home. But was it home? She'd never lived there. Her parents might call it home, but Ruby's home was the Lafferty homestead. Now that she was Azaria's apprentice, it would forever be her home. Someone in the maternal line always inherited that property, so why shouldn't it be Ruby?

She arrived at her parents' house, and was relieved to see Bella and Chandra sitting on the doorstep. Figuring Bella was not keen on the family meeting either, she smiled weakly.

"This sucks, doesn't it?" Ruby said, slinging her backpack to the ground.

"Do you get the feeling we've done something wrong?" Bella asked.

"Feels like it," Ruby agreed.

Eliza-May arrived, and said "Hey girls. Shall we go in together?"

James was sitting at the kitchen table, tumbler of rum to his right, and yellow legal pad to his left. Already, it contained a full page of notes.

"Come and sit down," he said, his face grim. "We need to talk."

He waited until they were seated, and didn't make eye contact even when Chandra gurgled and said "ba ba ba ba ba" followed by a giggle.

Sensing the gravity of the situation, Ruby tried to hold back her smile, but Chandra's wide eyes just ended up making her laugh. James thumped his fist against the table. "This family has fallen apart, and from today we're fixing it."

"With a glass of rum?" Eliza-May asked, sarcastically, still cringing at that night he fell asleep, drunk, on top of her. The stench still lingered in her nostrils.

"Enough! You're the reason we're in this state. If you'd just gotten a grip, Eliza-May, then we wouldn't be living here. You and your damn feeling sorry for yourself. If you had what it takes to move across country why didn't you use that energy to make our life in New York work for you? What's so special about this goddamn town anyway? It's boring! Hicksville. Full of hippies and no-hopers!"

Ruby and Bella looked at each other, not liking where this was going. Chandra started to fuss.

"I want Ruby and Bella to move back in with us. You can quit your job at that health store, and be a mother. You're not depressed now, so there's no reason you can't make meals each day and keep this family in order."

"I'm not moving back here!" Ruby said, standing up. "My home is with Gran and Great-Granny Car. I am NOT moving back here. Mom, tell him. Tell him how happy I am."

"And you can forget me moving back here. I'm not a child anymore. I'm a mother. I'm doing a great job. Everyone says so. I am staying right where I am. You can't make me move here. Mom? Say something!"

"James, you have a problem with me. Don't take it out on the girls." Eliza-May spoke calmly, hoping it would disguise her thumping heart.

"I want them home. There's no compromise on this. Don't you forget what I do for a living."

"What's that supposed to mean?" Eliza-May asked, her heart racing, her worst fears coming to the surface.

"I'll take out a court order if I have to against Azaria for holding my daughter up at that land, and if I have to, Bella, I'll get social welfare involved so that I can make sure you and your baby are here, and well cared for."

Bella screamed. "Have you gone crazy? What the hell is this about? You say you love me? I will never forget the day you found out I was pregnant. What did you say? You called me a low-life slut! That I was never going to make anything of my life. Well, let me tell you! I'm more happy, and more successful, than you will ever be. I have people in my life who actually want to be with me. And what do you have? Seriously, Dad, what do you actually have besides your own business and this expensive house that no one wants to live in?"

He stood up, and said "Don't you ever speak to me like that. Respect your elders!"

Ruby said "No wonder Mom fell in love with someone else. I can't blame her." She knew she shouldn't have said it, but that damn Luna was there urging her: "Say it, say it….Say it now!"

"What are you talking about? Eliza-May, what the hell does she mean?"

She closed her eyes. Everything around her was

falling apart, but the last thing she wanted for either of her daughters was for them to move in with a man who was becoming increasingly angry with life.

"It's true. I am in love with someone else. But, that's between me and him, and has nothing to do with whether or not the girls should live here. Let them go now, James. Let them go home."

Bella was crying. Chandra was screaming, her little body shaking with rage.

"Mom, why are you still here? If you love someone else, then go. Go! You don't owe Dad anything!" Bella yelled. "Please don't stay with him because of us."

James stalked across the room. "Shut up! Shut up! Chandra, stop screaming!" He bolted the front door, and connected the two security locks. "No one is leaving until this is sorted."

Ruby ran to the bathroom and pulled the phone out of her pocket. Her fingers were shaking so much she could barely make the call.

"Isaac, I need Gran," she wailed as he answered the phone.

"Ruby, you're hysterical. What's going on?"

"I want to come home now. Please, come quick. I'm scared." She locked the bathroom door, ignoring James's loud knocks.

"Come out, Ruby!" he yelled, banging on the door several times. "I am your father. I have a legal right to have you living under my roof!"

Isaac heard every word. "Ruby, we'll be there as quick as we can. Sweetie, stay safe." It broke his heart to hang up on her sobs.

"Dad, you're the problem here, not us. Look at you. You're the one who is causing this upset. Why don't you try changing and then we might want to be around you!" Bella had already texted Callum to drive over immediately. The only one who hadn't been able to make an SOS was Eliza-May. Mascara streaked down her cheeks. She could have been having a romantic stroll along the river with Clinton — the love of her life — but no, she was here, listening to a man who'd clearly had too much to drink and was hell-bent on getting his own way. She closed her eyes and prayed. *Please, someone help us.*

James pushed some pen and paper towards Eliza-May. "Here, write your resignation letter."

"No," she said firmly.

"Why should she?" Bella yelled. "She loves that job. It's the best thing that's happened to her in years. Why would you even want to take that away? It doesn't make sense. You're being cruel."

"I earn plenty of money. What does it say to the people of this town that my wife has to have a menial job in a health shop? It's ridiculous!" he said, slugging another gulp of rum. "Ridiculous!" he repeated, slamming his tumbler on the table.

"It's not menial. I'm at my happiest when I'm there. It's a fabulous place. Appleseeds is the hub of this community."

"You are coming home to look after this family." James stood up, and looked her firmly in the eyes. "You are leaving that job!"

"You don't get it, do you?" Bella said, drowned out by Chandra's cries. "No one wants to be with you. No one!"

James threw his glass against the wall, splintered shards piercing the carpet. "Stop talking to me like that! When did the women in this family become so rude? I won't have it. Start behaving properly!"

"Like you are?" Bella said, heading to the front door. "Let me out. You're keeping me here against my will. I'm almost 18 years old. You can't keep me here."

"Then you don't know the law very well! In Colorado the age of majority isn't until 18, so you can damn well live here until then."

"No. No I am not. And I'll fight you in court if I have to," Bella said.

"Who do you think you are?" James spat his words in disgust.

"Oh, I don't know, a low-life slut!" she yelled, with as much sarcasm as she could muster.

"You're certainly sounding like one!" he retorted.

"James, leave the girls alone," Eliza-May said calmly, trying to emulate Azaria's approach to life. "You want me to stay living here, and to stop seeing…" She nearly said Clinton's name, but decided against it. "I'll stay. I'll end my friendship. But let the girls go. I beg you."

"Mom, no! You've waited a long time for love, damn well grab it with both hands. Don't let Dad control you!" It didn't matter how loudly Bella yelled, it couldn't disguise the sobbing coming from the bathroom.

"I'm beginning legal action tomorrow." He sat down again, and then said "What shall we have for dinner?" It was the calm way in which he spoke, as if none of the previous conversation had just happened, which disturbed Eliza-May the most. Bella looked at her, her eyes questioning her mother, and wondering if they'd just hallucinated the past half an hour.

A loud knock at the front door shocked them all.

"Who the hell is visiting us at dinner time?" James asked.

"It's Callum. He's taking me home. Let him in Dad, or he'll call the police."

James looked at her in disgust. "How could you betray me like this?"

"I don't know what's happened to you, Dad, but you need help. Real help."

"Mom, can we give you a lift somewhere? To Gran's house?" Bella asked, heading to the front door when the knocking came again, more forcefully. "Mom?"

Eliza-May looked desperately at Bella. "I'll stay with Ruby."

"Ruby can come with us. We can all go. Mom! Go and get her! Dad, open this damn door!" Bella yelled.

"You'll regret this defiance. The law is bigger than you, Bella. Much bigger. It'll flatten you like an insect on a windshield. Mark my words. You don't have a chance."

"It may well be, but I also believe in justice. Open the god-damn door before I scream as loudly as Chandra!"

"Bella?" Isaac called from the other side. "Bella, are you locked in?"

James unlocked the door and avoided eye contact with Isaac.

Eliza-May convinced Ruby to come out of the bathroom. She ran straight to Azaria's arms. "Take me home, Gran. I want to go home."

Rum lingered in the air, a silent witness to a disintegrating family. Azaria knew that whatever had transpired in this room had traumatised them. She could feel herself shaking.

"Mom?" Bella called from the outside steps. "Please come with us. Stay at the flat with me and Callum. Do not stay here."

"Love, do you want to come to our house tonight?" Azaria asked softly.

Eliza-May was torn. The last thing she wanted was to be here with James, but she wasn't sure if leaving him on his own, in this state, was the best thing to do.

Knowing how far Eliza-May had come in the past year, Azaria wanted to do her best to ensure her life just kept getting better. "Come with us, honey."

"I need to pack some clothes for work," Eliza-May said, hesitating, still unsure if what had just transpired was real or a dream.

"Okay, no problem. I'll come and help you," Azaria said, sensing that she needed more than moral support.

James sat on the sofa, flicking on the 24-hour news.

Azaria tilted her head to Isaac, motioning to get Ruby in the car.

Bella fell into Callum's arms, her whole body convulsing in shock. Isaac recognised the signs and raced to the car and got a blanket.

"Help me wrap her in this, Callum," he said urgently. "Ruby, grab the baby. Now!"

Isaac ripped off his coat, and placed that around her too. "What the hell happened in there? Never mind. Don't answer that yet. We need to get you home. Bella, do you want to come to ours or go back to your flat?"

Callum replied for her, "We'll be fine at the flat. But, could you guys come with us for a bit? Just till I know she's okay?"

"Of course." Isaac nodded.

Azaria and Eliza-May came outside, suitcases in hand.

"Right, Callum, I'll see you at your place in a few minutes. Put the heating on full in the car, okay?" Isaac said.

"Yep."

A Story To Tell

The past few days had changed Starr's life in so many ways. Meeting Mahina, and the friendship that was developing between them, had only highlighted that everyone has a story to tell. Her syndicated articles felt so far away right now, and in other ways she felt like she was living them every single moment just from within her own family. When she'd received Azaria's missive about the blow-up with James, Starr felt jolted back to reality. It was fun hanging out with her new cousin, but it was time to go home. And, perhaps, it was time to head back to Australia. She'd done her job: she'd found Astrid's daughter, and now it was up to Mahina how the rest of the story was told.

Mahina begged Starr to stay one more day. "Come to the studio with me. I'm putting down a couple of tracks for my new album. Let me prove to you that I have a job and don't just sit around here eating Carnell's food all day long!" she laughed.

"Now that's an offer I can't refuse. I'd love to come. Thank you!"

Starr couldn't remember the last time she'd had so much fun. Hanging out with Mahina in the studio as she put down tracks was surreal. The familiar faces of country-music stars were just part of Mahina's everyday work life, but for Starr, it was a dream come true. They had lunch with Carrie Underwood, and late-afternoon coffee with Garth Brooks. Nothing could surpass that moment, though, when Mahina asked Starr if she'd join the three backing singers on one of her recordings. What she'd have done to be able to put a note on Twitter that she was recording with the great Mahina Safiya! It was a day that she'd remember for the rest of her life.

"I need to go home now. There's a whole lot going on, and I'd like to be there for my Mom for a bit before I go back to Australia. I know I can't make you meet Astrid. I understand your reasons, and yes, a lot of it for her is about erasing the guilt, but she's still your mother, and when she dies you'll never get the chance to talk to her again. Death is final. You know that, Mahina. I'm not telling you anything new, but I do hope you'll reconsider, if not for her sake, then for yours. Time is of the essence."

"It's been good meeting you, cuz! Keep in touch, hey? I'm doing some concerts in Oz early next year. I'll send you some tickets!"

"Backstage passes?" Starr squealed.

"Of course!"

They hugged long and slow, and they rocked from side to side, as they cried their goodbyes.

"Drive safe," Mahina said, wiping her tears.

Starr nodded, and walked to her car. And then she remembered. "Ah, there's something I meant to give you." She reached into her backpack and pulled out the old journal. "This is yours. Before you say anything, please don't get cross. I know it was wrong to take it, but it felt more wrong to leave it behind."

Mahina smiled. "You brought this back for me?" recognising the cover instantly.

"You're not angry?" Starr asked.

"It was the one thing I really missed when I left, but I've never had the heart to go back to the lighthouse. Thank you, Starr. I mean it. Hey, who knows, maybe I'll even write a song about us!"

Starr drove away, tears streaming down her cheeks, soft sobs interfering with the song she was singing. Of all the things she was certain of in this world, she knew this:

her family would love Mahina! "Horse to water, and all that," she told herself as the car veered around the cedar trees into the driveway lined with yellow poplars.

Unsettled

There was an eerie silence in the Lafferty homestead for the next few days. Everyone was reeling from that evening at James's house. Azaria wondered if James would keep his threat to take legal action to have his girls back home. She couldn't understand why he'd go to such lengths when most of the time he wasn't even at home. Was it just a power game? Did he feel so out of control that he had to resort to legal tactics? In all the years she'd known him, she'd never seen this cruel side of him before. She knew — they all knew — that when it came to his career he was ruthless, but at home? No, but then, if she was honest, he never did spend much time there. It would destroy Ruby to leave the homestead. She'd spent ages getting her bedroom just right, and was devoted to helping Azaria in the barn each afternoon, developing her skills, learning her vocation.

And as for Bella's life: she was living as an adult in every sense of the word. What right did James have to change that and suggest she wasn't a good-enough mother? Bella's mothering instincts were strong; that was obvious for all to see.

Azaria shook her head. And then a force from deep within the pit of her belly rose like an unstoppable volcano. Everything that ever mattered to her in this lifetime culminated in that moment: *she would fight for her family*. If it came to it, she'd fight for Ruby in court no matter what the cost or consequence. An anger that she had never experienced before in her life tore through her body. Yes, James was their father. She understood that, but what she couldn't accept was that he was doing this for their good.

Martin and Kara felt out of place, having arrived into a psychological cold-war zone that neither was prepared for, and found themselves spending more and more time on Astrid and Bob's land, living in their own little world, and enjoying taking long walks together. When they did go to Azaria's, most of their time was spent outdoors in the fresh, uncomplicated air. It was a peaceful afternoon, that sunny Saturday, when she showed him all around the 700 acres: all the places she played as a child; where she lost her first tooth; where her father was killed by a tree in a storm, and how she found his body; where she had her first kiss...

"It seems to me like you haven't been kissed in a while, Kara, if you don't mind me saying so."

"How do you know, and why would I mind?" she asked, flirting slightly.

When she left William that frightful day in New York — a day that seemed a lifetime ago now — she vowed never again to have a relationship. What was she doing spending so much time hanging out with Martin? Weren't all men the same? Well, apart from Isaac, Bob, and Callum?

"I'd like to kiss you," he said, reaching out for her hand. "Would you object?"

"I'll have to think about that," she said, smiling brightly.

"Don't take too long, then, I've already waited for what seems like weeks."

"And here I was thinking it had been months," she laughed.

"So, that's a yes, then?"

She squeezed his hand tighter, beckoning him to come closer. "What do you think?" she smiled.

"I think I'm about to burst with happiness. Come here."

She expected him to reach down and kiss her, but instead he scooped her up into his arms and carried her out of the meadow to a copse of trees. He placed her down carefully, and took off his coat for them to sit on.

"You're really staying in the area, then?" he asked in disbelief. "You're sure you're not going to head back to Zululand?"

"I'm sure. Martin, you're talking too much. Shhhh."

"I just want to make sure we're both in this together…that…"

"What?"

"That you're not going to break my heart." He said the words ever so softly, but felt the gravity heavy as lead.

"As long as you promise not to break mine then I think we should both be fine. But, I am committed to being here." She reached over and traced his strong jawline. "Are you going to kiss me then?"

He laughed gently, bringing her to the ground. "Did you really think I'd forgotten?"

It was the tender way Martin looked into her eyes for the longest time that really spoke to her. "I feel like I've always known you," he said softly, "and it scares me a bit."

"Why?"

"Because if I've always known you, then what am I waiting for?"

"I was about to ask that very same question," she laughed, brushing her lips against his. "I would like you to kiss me. Do you think it might happen today?" she giggled. "Or tomorrow, maybe?" she asked, gently tickling him.

"How about now?"

Martin didn't wait for her to answer. Soft and sweet, his kisses erased every painful experience of her life. Melting into his touch, she found herself crying. So this is what happens when destiny finds you, she thought, grateful she had come home.

"Have I upset you? Did I hurt you?" he asked when her tears wet his cheeks.

"Just shut up and kiss me," she said, crying, laughing, pulling him closer.

For quite some time they kissed, giggled, and smiled at each other, not quite believing they'd reached this point. They made love slowly and tenderly that Autumn afternoon, there beneath the Juniper trees, the sweet scent of honey from the hives wafting in the breeze. The chill in the air didn't deter them. Woodsmoke from the homestead drifted their way, reminding them that they weren't alone.

For some time they simply lay together, there in each other's arms, to hell with the rest of the world, but as day eased away and night-time beckoned, Martin whispered "You're shivering. Best get back to the madhouse, hey?"

A Time of Reckoning

The postman passed a handful of mail to Azaria as she sat on the porch swing with Car. She flipped through them, pulling out all the personal ones first. She read some out to Car, and they laughed together at the news from various friends. The bills were opened and assorted in due-date order.

It was the last one — she knew what it was immediately, of course, by the court-house envelope — that she opened reluctantly.

A court date had been set for James Megane to seek the return of his daughters from the Lafferty Homestead and the flat above Appleseeds health store. James had filed a suit against Azaria and Isaac.

Azaria read it to herself, then gave the piece of paper to Car. They passed each other a look of resignation.

"It will all sort itself out in the wash, darling," Car said wisely. "Don't let it take up too much of your mind. It's unlikely a judge would rule in his favour."

"But he's their father!"

"Yes, that's true, but those girls aren't toddlers. They're feisty young women with minds of their own. Trust the process to unfold as it should."

"I wish I had your confidence, Ma. This is twisting me inside out. I never planned for Rubes to move in here. And I certainly wasn't trying to take Bella away from her family. Don't you remember the state they were in when she got pregnant? Eliza-May unable to lift her head from the pillow or even open her curtains; and James always unavailable. I was just trying to be helpful."

"Honey, I'm the last person you need to explain anything to. Those girls have thrived since being here.

And that is exactly why I'm telling you not to fret. I can't stop you from worrying about the outcome, but you of all people know how to take things in your stride. Why should this be any different?"

Azaria started to cry. "It is different! *I'm* different. I've lost a child. Everything about me is different now. I'm raw and aching. It might not look like it to the rest of the world, but I go through every day feeling like the walking wounded! Rubes and Bella will never take Luna's place. No one could. But more than anything, I don't want to lose them. They give me hope on those darkest of days. And when I see little Chandra's smile it reminds me that I have a reason to go on."

"Sweetheart, you have a million reasons to go on."

"I know. I know. It's just…sometimes I feel so guilty when I have a good day, you know? When Isaac makes me laugh, or Rubes wraps her skinny little arms around my waist as she asks for another piece of chocolate cake, or seeing Eliza-May looking so radiant after all these years. I've lost one daughter, but gained another. I never thought I'd get Eliza-May back. I have these moments of wondering how I deserve such joy when a part of me has been crushed forever."

"Tragedy shapes us, honey, but it doesn't have the right to hold us hostage. Let yourself enjoy all the precious moments that come to you. Don't shut your heart down to all the years of love still ahead." Car reached for her daughter's hand.

Azaria nodded in acknowledgement at Car's words. Tears stung her eyes.

"My beautiful daughter, come here," Car said, giving her a hug. "I know you've changed. Luna's death hurt all of us. But there's something about you that you obviously can't see for yourself: you're like a sunflower. No matter how dark and grey the day is, you stand tall and beautiful reaching for the light; your brightness is a beacon for everyone around you. James might be wielding his power through the legal system, but no one is as powerful as you, Azaria Linden."

Where Are You?

Car pottered around the garden, deheading some of the last blossoms. Today was the first time in a while that she'd had the place to herself. Ah, peace! The calm was comforting after all the ragged emotions of recent weeks. She looked across the valley, breathing in the beautiful view, and giving thanks for the wonderful life she'd had on this mountain. *It's a good day to die*, she smiled, feeling the Autumn sunlight on her face. For a while now, she'd dreamt of Luna every night. The dreams were comforting, and Car concluded that her granddaughter was calling her Home.

"Okay, my darling. I'm ready. If it's my time, then so be it. It's been a good life. I'd have liked to meet Mahina, but if it's not meant to be, then I can accept that. But there's one thing I have to do first."

It had been about eight years since Car had last been to the hot spring. The trek could be quite treacherous, and they'd never been able to navigate a different path due to thick woodlands and rugged rocks. She was determined to soak in those medicinal waters one last time. She knew Azaria would be reluctant to let her go, and so she decided not to ask anyone's permission. Heading inside to grab a towel and flask of water, Car smiled at her plan. She felt decidedly mischievous, knowing full well how Azaria would react, but after the tension of recent weeks Car knew it would do her the world of good. Besides, Azaria wouldn't be back for hours, so that gave Car plenty of time to have a long soak, and then take her time getting back up the hill.

As she walked along the path, remembering all the landmarks, small and large, Car couldn't help smiling.

This property was priceless. So many amazing memories: births, marriages, families, untold fabulous meals. Yes, there'd been deaths, too. But somehow, through it all, the family held together.

It took much longer to reach the spring than it used to but she was proud of herself for every single step, and for managing to arrive safely. Undressing, Car looked down at her naked body. It was a vessel that had grown two beautiful babies. She rested her hands gently across her belly, and prayed to her God. "Look after my daughters and their families. Keep them safe for me."

The air, cool against her skin, induced goosebumps. Stepping into the warm waters, Car sighed. "Ah, this is what I've been missing from my life."

For two hours, Car soaked in the water, letting her cares wash away. If she was honest, the idea of James Megane dragging her family through court terrified her, but she knew that if she gave it too much thought it would become a reality. In her mind, she saw the situation being resolved in such a way that Bella could still stay living autonomously, and Ruby would spend her days indefinitely at the homestead. She saw them, that moment in her mind's eye: years from now, all gathered on the veranda, laughing, celebrating Chandra's tenth birthday. That was her hope. This was the dream.

"What's wrong?" Isaac asked when he came into the kitchen.

Azaria put down her stirring spoon against the pan, and said "I can't find Car. I've been up to the hives, looked in the barn, went to the orchard. She's nowhere around here. I've rung up her friends in case someone picked her up for an outing. No one's seen her. Astrid and I were only at Healing Waters for an hour, then we popped into town and came back. I'm getting worried."

Ruby listened attentively, then went into the garden and picked a handful of flowers before heading to her bedroom.

"I'll grab Bob and we'll look around the land again. Where do you think she'd go?" Isaac asked.

"I've no idea. There weren't any jobs I asked her to do. She'd brought the washing in, and baked some cookies. But there's no sign of her. We need to move fast."

"Stay here," Isaac said, heading to the barn to find Bob.

"Bob, Car's missing," Isaac said. "I need your help. Do you want to bring Astrid to the house to stay with Azaria? We're going to need torches at this rate. Sun's going down fast."

"We'll be right there. Do you want me to call anyone else?" Bob asked.

"I'll call Martin and Kara up, but we best head off now."

Ruby sat on her bed, the plucked flower petals before her. Closing her eyes, she held her hand over them for a few minutes, and asked "Where will we find Great-Granny Car?"

She'd taken to reading flowers on most days now: seeing images formed from their scattered petals; and listening to any accompanying voices, and sometimes, on rare occasions, seeing images. Luna was there, quick as a flash: *Down by the spring. She's fallen.*

"No, Luna. She doesn't go down there, it's not safe. Tell me the truth!"

"Down near the spring," Luna insisted.

Ruby was angry. Why would Luna say that? Everyone knew that Car didn't go down that track.

But what else could she do? Azaria was frantic with worry, and it was getting dark. Maybe she could find out for herself and not have to look like an idiot for even suggesting Car would do something as foolish as take a walk to the spring.

Isaac, Martin and Bob headed off around the property looking in all the obvious places. Azaria and Kara went through the buildings again.

Ruby waited till they were all out of sight, then grabbed a torch and headed down the hill. Darkness had set over the mountains now, and the baying of a wolf scared her. But she had to find Car. She couldn't leave her out in the dark alone. Car needed her. It was some time later, when she arrived at the spring, disheartened to discover that Car was nowhere to be seen. She called her name, then started crying.

"You lied to me aunty Luna! You lied. I believed in you! How can I do flower readings if you don't speak to me clearly? I thought you said she was at the spring? I'm here, and she's nowhere to be seen!"

A horrible thought occurred to Ruby. What if Car had been here, and perhaps drowned? With all her willpower, Ruby brought the torchlight over the water expecting to see her great-grandmother at the bottom. But she wasn't there. She wasn't anywhere.

The walk up the hill seemed to take so much longer than the trek down. Ruby was becoming increasingly furious with Luna's voice in her ear saying "Go back! Go back down!"

She arrived at the homestead to find everyone gathered on the veranda.

"Where have you been, Ruby?" Azaria demanded. "One missing person is more than I can bear right now."

Ruby started to cry. Isaac wrapped his arms around her. "What is it, Rubes?"

"Luna told me Car was at the spring. I went to find her, but I couldn't," she cried, squeezing him tighter. "I couldn't find her, and Luna kept telling me to go back. I was scared, and there was a wolf, and it's so dark when you're by yourself."

"Okay, okay. You say Luna said she's by the spring?"

"Uh huh." Ruby sobbed.

"Okay, come on guys, let's go back down there. Ruby, stay with Azaria and Kara," he said firmly.

"Hang on a minute," Azaria called. "Luna is dead. Luna couldn't possibly know where Car is."

Astrid turned to look at her sister in disbelief.

"This from the person who uses a crystal to find water?" She turned to Isaac. "Go, Isaac. Bob, Martin, go!"

Isaac turned to Ruby. "You should tell your Gran about your conversations with Luna. Get inside. Stay warm."

For two hours, Astrid, Kara and Azaria watched in amazement as Ruby 'read' the flower petals. They each took turns asking questions, while Ruby divined the answer.

Astrid's question was perhaps the most obvious: "Will I meet my daughter?"

"Luna says you will, but you need to be patient."

Azaria asked "Will I get to keep Ruby here with us?"

Ruby laughed, "Oh Gran, you don't need to ask the flowers that. There's no way in hell anyone's making me leave here. Ever."

"Ask anyway," Azaria encouraged, doubt creeping in at the edges.

Luna replied, her voice soft in Ruby's ear: "You will always have Ruby with you in your heart."

Azaria was alarmed. What did that actually mean?

"Aunty Kara, do you have another question?" Ruby asked.

Kara was desperate to ask, but so far she'd kept her feelings for Martin under wraps, or at least so she thought.

"Don't you want to ask about you and Martin?" Astrid teased.

"How do you know?" Kara asked, incredulous.

"Everyone knows!" Azaria laughed.

Her relief was palpable. "My question is: Will this relationship last?"

Ruby cried softly when she heard Luna's reply. "Throughout all of time."

Kara brushed the tears off her cheeks. "Will the men find Car?"

Ruby asked the question, scattering the flowers on the cloth. Before she had time to listen to Luna's reply, there was a commotion on the veranda. They ran out to find three burly men, and one frail lady.

"Let's get her in the warm," Isaac said, coaxing them inside.

"She's fine, love, she's fine. Cold and shaken. Come on Car, let's get you by the fire. Rubes, put the kettle on. Kara, can you get some blankets out here?"

Azaria looked on as he fired instructions like a drill sergeant. Car was alive, and appeared unhurt.

"Mom? Where were you?" Azaria asked, her upset clearly visible.

"Oh honey, I had the best time today. I'd forgotten how wonderful that hot pool is…it was just what I needed."

"Seriously? You went down that hill without anyone to help you?"

"The getting down was a piece of cake. The getting back up, not so much."

Isaac continued. "She fell. It was quite a drop. It's a miracle we found her. Frankly, we'd have given up if it wasn't for Luna."

Azaria's face crumpled. "Don't ever do that to us again."

"Don't scold me. Just remember, I'm your mother. It's not the other way around," Car smiled.

"You frightened me. You frightened all of us. If you really want to go to the spring, then please take someone with you. Promise me that?"

"It's not the same though, is it? Being on your own in that water is an entirely different experience."

Azaria shook her head. "I'll handcuff you to this house if I have to!"

They all laughed, and Ruby brought Car some sweetened vanilla chai tea. "Gran?" she said, looking at Azaria, "I noticed some chocolate cake in the pantry. Is it for a special reason?"

Azaria smirked. "I thought I'd hidden that cake!"

"You always hide things behind the big drum of olive oil. I know that, so it's not really hiding is it?"

The Old Woman Speaks

Car Lafferty sat in James Megane's office, her eyes piercing into his as if they were silent, stainless-steel pins holding down a dead butterfly. She had to acknowledge this part of herself — the cold-hearted scientist examining a specimen — if she had any hope of understanding James.

Tomorrow the family would face him in court. She'd promised herself that she wouldn't interfere, but as the day drew nearer, Car realised she couldn't just sit back and pray. She had to move her feet, too. He returned her stare, unwilling to communicate; but time was money, and he had three clients waiting.

"It's not appropriate for you to be here, Car. We can discuss the situation tomorrow in court, in front of a judge. They're my children. End of story. I'd appreciate it if you'd leave this to the legal system. I'm busy."

"What are you trying to achieve, James?" she asked tenderly, hoping to appeal to his more human side even though he was in full legal mode. "You know those girls are happy. Both of them. They're thriving. You can't deny that. Who are you trying to hurt the most? You'll alienate those girls forever if you go ahead with this."

"I don't see that this is any of your business, Car." His tone was abrupt.

"It became my business when the girls moved to Colorado because their parents were unavailable. Azaria and I have invested our time and love into making sure they felt settled, secure and appreciated. Of course it's my business!" She felt her blood boiling, and consciously calmed her breath. Car didn't want to get caught in a war, and knew the only hope of getting him to see sense was to find her centre. To be calm.

"I didn't ask either of you to interfere! Damn it. This is all Eliza-May's fault, not mine. If she'd have just stopped feeling sorry for herself, we wouldn't be in this situation right now. Car, leave."

"Depression is a mental illness, James. Haven't you learnt anything about what she experienced?"

"Eliza-May didn't make an effort to fit into New York. Look at her now! If she'd have done that years ago, we wouldn't be here having this conversation."

"But we *are* here having this conversation. And I'm asking you to rethink this course of action. If this is about Eliza-May being in love with another man, then you'll have to be a man yourself and take it in your stride. This has nothing whatsoever to do with your girls."

"Who the hell is she 'in love' with?" he asked in a mocking tone, his fingers acting like quotation marks.

"That's irrelevant. What you need to understand is that the issue is between you and Eliza-May, and putting those girls through a court case isn't going to make you a better father, or earn their respect. Quite the opposite."

"Tell me who she's in love with, and I'll drop the court order," he said, avoiding eye contact and heading over to a filing cabinet.

Shit, she muttered under her breath. This was not the path she wanted to go down. Car didn't want to lie, but she also knew that if she mentioned Clinton's name that James was just as likely to head straight to the bookshop and punch him in the face. She opted for lying, crossed her old gnarled knuckles, and reluctantly activated the ever-present arthritis.

"Jack? Jack someone, I think? I can't be sure. Wasn't really paying attention," she fibbed, picking at some loose thread on her hand-knitted poncho.

"Car, you have one chance: give me his full name by nine tomorrow morning, or this goes ahead. No ifs, no buts. And don't bloody lie to me. No one in your family is capable of lying convincingly."

Car picked up her small basket.

"I don't like being blackmailed," she said quietly.

Turning on the Light

Mahina paced the lounge room, then headed to the kitchen where Carnell was preparing lunch.

"Are you okay, Miss Safiya? You just haven't been the same since your cousin left," he said.

"I'm not okay. I don't know what to do. I want to meet the rest of my family, but I feel like my mother only wants to see me because she's dying. She's had more than forty years to find me. That's a long time to not show interest in someone. Why should I see her?"

"For yourself. Do it for you. Once she's gone, you won't have any more chances."

"But...what if...she doesn't like me? What if I'm a disappointment to her? What if we just don't get each other's vibe? I mean, mothers and daughters are supposed to have this amazing bond, but we don't have anything. Nothing. She's some random stranger to me. Why should we get together?"

"Because if you don't, then you'll never know. Bernice and Steven were strangers to you. And look how much you grew to love each other. That was without the benefit of shared blood. Give it a chance, girl. You've got nothing to lose. It's not like she's going to take your millions."

"That is true." She kept pacing. "I might go to the lighthouse first. I think I need to revisit that part of my life before I can go back to the beginning."

"Sounds like a plan. When are you going?"

"This week might be a good time. I can't do any recording till my voice is sorted. I'm really angry. Three doctors have said there's nothing wrong with my throat, but I can feel it. I just can't hit my bottom four notes."

Carnell wrote down a number. "Why don't you visit Jenna Adams? I know she has a reputation as being a white witch around Nashville, but my mother swears by her homeopathy. Don't look at me like that!" Carnell chuckled. "Try her. She's trustworthy, don't worry. All the celebrities go to her. Tell her it's urgent. Sometimes she keeps a few slots open for emergencies."

The office of Jenna Adams was all-white décor, filled with lush palms and rubber plants. For forty-five minutes, Jenna talked through Mahina's symptoms.

"So, has anything different happened in your life this year. Any big changes? I appreciate you must always be busy, but I'm talking about something out of the ordinary."

"This is confidential, right?" Mahina asked. The last thing she wanted was her private life splashed across a tabloid.

"100% in the vault. What is said here, stays here."

Mahina shared her story, about Starr's visit, and how it unleashed so many powerful feelings about the life she'd always known, and the shock of discovering her birth mother was alive.

"You're angry at her?" Jenna probed.

"Yes. I'm furious. I have a wonderful life. I've had pain in my past, but that's where it is. Here, now, my life... it's wonderful. I don't want that to change. How dare she just think she can ask for my forgiveness because she's suddenly staring at the Pearly Gates!"

"Maybe it's taken her all this time to find the courage. It's possible she was worried you might reject her."

"You mean like she rejected me when I was born?" Mahina snapped.

"Yes. Is that what you're doing? Are you punishing

191

her?" asked Jenna.

Mahina stood up and walked around the room. "I'm not that sort of person. I'm not mean, I'm kind. I hate the feelings this is bringing up for me. But yes, I'm punishing her."

"Who do you think is suffering the most?" Jenna asked.

"I don't understand what any of this has to do with why I can't sing."

"Your energy is locked in your throat. It's the most powerful part of you. It's what has made you who you are today. But if you can't communicate your feelings, no matter how angry you are, then your voice isn't going to heal in a hurry. Tell your mother how you feel. Express your anger, and how rejected you felt knowing that she gave you away."

"I can't tell a dying woman that," Mahina cried, rushing out of the room.

Bad Timing

Each night after work, Eliza-May and Clinton would head upstairs to his office at A Novel Idea. For the next hour, they'd share a bite to eat, and talk about their day. She'd spend her nights on the sofa above Appleseeds in Bella's flat or over at Azaria's. She refused to return to James's house, despite him sending flowers to her workplace each day, and buying his lunch from Appleseeds. Not once did she sleep at Clinton's house, though her arms ached to be held by him all night long. Each day she promised that soon she would officially leave James.

"I know this situation is difficult, but you can't let him bully you like this." Clinton said firmly.

"I'm scared of what he'll do to the girls' lives if I file for divorce. I'm still their mother, and I have to put their needs ahead of mine."

Clinton unwrapped their evening meal, but as soon as he placed it on the table in front of Eliza-May, she ran from the room. Racing downstairs after her, he found her bent over the toilet. Watching her vomit so violently, Clinton wondered if she needed to go to hospital. Squatting down behind her, he gently rubbed her back and passed some toilet paper to her.

"I'm so sorry. I didn't know you were feeling ill. Why didn't you say something?" he asked.

"It's just a little bug. I'm sure it'll pass." Eliza-May wiped her mouth.

"How long have you felt like this?"

"About a week or two." She slung back on her haunches. "I feel awful. Can you take me home?"

"Sure. Er, where's home for you these days?" he asked, somewhat confused.

"Can you take me to your place?" she pleaded, surprising both of them.

Clinton kissed the top of her head, and smiled. "Of course. Wait by the back door while I get the car from the car park."

She nodded.

Clinton helped Eliza-May shower, and as they lay in bed together that night, she declared: "I want to spend every night with you. I'm sick of this sneaking around. This is the life I want. To be here."

"That's what I want too. I know I said I'm prepared to be patient, and don't get me wrong, because I am, but I am finding this increasingly frustrating. Do you know how much I want to make love to you right now? But I won't. I can't. Not while things are like this." He held her tightly.

"I'm going to be sick!" she said, diving out of bed and just making it to the bathroom in time.

The Truth

When Starr phoned with the news that she was half an hour away from the homestead, Bob left the building work, even though it was only noon, and told Isaac to pack up the tools for the day. He wanted to be with Astrid to hear whatever the news was. It was obvious that Starr was on her own, so there'd be that disappointment to deal with before anything else.

An hour later, gathered at the old farmhouse table, Azaria served up lunch: a heaping salad of green leaves, feta cubes, cherry tomatoes, cucumber slices, alfalfa sprouts and grated carrot; sweet potato fries with smoked paprika, and red-bean chilli.

There was an unusual silence in the kitchen as everyone waited for Starr to speak.

"I'm sorry that your daughter isn't here with me at this moment, aunty Astrid, but I have faith that she will come to visit."

Astrid hung her head low. "Time isn't on my side, sweetheart. Thank you for all you've done. If she wanted to be here, she would."

"It's not that simple. You've had a lifetime thinking about her, and more recently adjusting to the idea of meeting her again. She's just found out, and has spent her life believing both parents were dead. To find out that you're alive was enough of a shock. To find out that you're dying only adds to that. And somewhere between those two pieces of information she is questioning why you've never looked for her before. She's an only child, and this family that she is more than likely to walk into is huge. There are so many of us. You can't blame her for being a bit intimidated. I would be!"

"She's right," Bob said, "absolutely right. We have to trust your daughter will come when she's ready."

"But I don't have time!" Astrid cried.

They ate in relative silence, and Azaria found herself wishing that Ruby wasn't at school that day. She'd almost certainly say something to make them laugh or see the bright side of the situation.

"So, her name is Mahina, which, believe it or not means: Moon."

Astrid shook her head, and then gave out a little laugh. "Of course it does. Just so you all know: she's *my* daughter, not Azaria's, right?"

The mood lightened a little with her laughter.

Starr continued: "Safiya means: the sea."

"Mahina Safiya?" Azaria asked. "Isn't there a country music singer you're obsessed with who has that name? You know, that one you and Luna have been raving about for years."

"One and the same," Starr said, biting her lip at the reality of how easy it was for people to assume they know someone just because they're famous. "She hasn't had the greatest childhood. Mahina spent 12 years in an orphanage run by a convent, and was then adopted swiftly by an older couple who ran a lighthouse. She had four fantastic years with them, and really grew to love them and life by the ocean. I've been there. I've seen her room. It's an amazing place. Not all was bad in her childhood. She was loved."

"She left home at sixteen?" Astrid asked.

Starr sighed. "Her parents — her adoptive parents — lost their lives one night in a storm. The light in the lighthouse stopped working and they had to man the cliffs with nothing but lanterns. They slipped over the edge."

"No," whispered Azaria, Isaac holding her hand.

Starr nodded. "Mahina saw the lanterns in the dark as they tumbled down into the rocks below. She was powerless to help. After the funeral, she left the area and changed her name. She needed a fresh start, and moved to Nashville. She'd already learnt to play the guitar and was an avid songwriter. But," she continued, "she's an intensely private person, and getting to know her wasn't easy. She's lovely, though. You'll love her, Astrid. I promise you. All of you will," she said, looking around the table to Azaria, Car, Isaac, Bob and Astrid. "I felt a real connection with her, and I know she felt it with me. That's why I'm begging you to be patient. She'll come."

"Okay," Bob replied reassuringly. "We asked you to help find her, and you've done that. Mahina knows where we are. We can't ask more of you than that."

"So what do we do in the meantime?" Astrid asked.

Azaria replied in an instant. "You keep working on your dream: build that residential home. Put your energy into that and into looking after yourself. They're both full-time jobs, Astrid."

Isaac opened the door of the Aga and pulled out a pear, coconut, and chocolate crumble.

"That smells amazing," Car said, placing bowls onto the table. "I think this calls for a celebration. Thank you Starr for bringing us such fantastic news." She turned to Astrid. "This *is* brilliant news."

"Yes, Ma," Astrid agreed, putting a lid on her disappointment.

Scales of Justice

Azaria, Isaac, Car, Eliza-May, Ruby, Bella, Chandra and Callum were gathered at the front of the town's tiny courthouse. Car couldn't stand it any longer. "I went to see James yesterday," she said reluctantly, "and he said that he'd stop the court case if I told him who you were in love with, Eliza-May. I didn't tell him, but…I just don't want your family to go through all this. It's not necessary. His issue is with you, not the girls."

"Mom, you have to tell him," Ruby begged.

"Please, Mom?" Bella asked, gripping Callum's hand for support.

Appleseeds was closed for the day, and Isaac was by Azaria's side. "If that's all it takes, it's a small price to pay, but I can understand your reluctance, Eliza-May. This is a small town. Clinton's a great guy. Everyone loves him, but you know what gossip is like."

"I can't. It's not fair to Clinton. It could ruin his business if James put his mind to smearing his name."

"And your daughters?" Azaria asked. "What about them? The court will examine every detail of their lives."

"Hello Clinton," Isaac said, seeing him approach the family from behind.

"Clinton?" Eliza-May asked, "What are you doing here?"

"I'm not letting you go through this alone. I know you have your family, but I want to support you. I don't want us to hide anymore."

"He'll destroy you, Clinton. Honestly, he will." Eliza-May wiped the tears from her eyes.

"I'm prepared for that. Don't underestimate my ability to look after myself," he said gently, his finger lifting her chin so that she'd look into his eyes.

"James wants to know who Eliza-May is in love with, and says he'll stop the court case if we tell him who it is," Car confessed.

"Okay. Let's do it," Clinton agreed.

"You don't know what you're agreeing to," Eliza-May cried.

"Shhhh," Ruby whispered as she saw her father approaching, but it was too late.

"So, this is your love interest," James snickered in Clinton's direction. "See you in court!"

"Hang on a minute," Car said, demanding an explanation. "You said if you knew who he was that you wouldn't go ahead."

"No, I said if *you* told me who it was that I wouldn't go ahead. Big difference, Car."

Azaria sat in the stuffy court room, her mind turning to Eliza-May's wedding day and how James had been devoted to her, but insisted on skipping the honeymoon so he could return to work. She went alone. Perhaps the writing was already on the wall then. She thought about when Bella and Ruby were born, and all the late-night calls when Eliza-May would cry down the phone because it was after midnight and her husband still wasn't home from the office. Eventually the nightly calls became weekly, then monthly, even though he was still out seven nights a week. And then, the phone stopped ringing at all. Azaria often flew to New York just to check on Eliza-May, but there was very little she could do to rectify the situation. From a distance, she watched their marriage wither to an arid arrangement where they were held together only in name. But this? This day in court? Was that the best that could come out of their marriage? Surely there was another way?

Silently offering a prayer to the Egyptian Goddess Maat, she asked for justice, fairness and integrity to reign. Imagining the scales of justice evenly balanced, Azaria visualised everyone's needs being met fairly, and for the situation to be resolved quickly. On one side of her, Isaac squeezed her hand; and on the other, Car was there, holding her hand and patting it gently with the other.

James stood up and put forward his case for reclaiming full custody of his children, and explained that he didn't feel their current influences were in their best interests. Azaria closed her ears and heart to his digs at her lifestyle and Earth-loving tendencies, and Bella just laughed it off when he said she was a child and needed someone to look after her.

Eliza-May was called to the stand and asked why her daughters were not in her care. She felt uncomfortable reliving her years of depression, with Clinton there watching, but as she made eye contact she could see that he wasn't sitting in judgement, but looking at her with nothing but love. Feeling a bit freer, she said how different her life was now, and that her girls were more than welcome to live with her but that she could see how happy and settled they were in their new homes, and she had no wish to interrupt that for them. Her door, she said, was always open, and that they knew that.

The judge read through all the arguments for both sides, and asked to have more time to consider his decision. He called Ruby and Bella to the stand, asking them to explain their current living situations and what had brought them to this point. He put in a request for Ruby's school teachers to provide a report of her progress, and said he wanted to see statements from Bella's healthcare provider.

By 4pm, everyone was exhausted. The judge set a new date but ordered that the girls remain in their current situation until that point. If they wished to see their father in the meantime, that was entirely their decision.

There was a collective sigh of relief from Azaria's side of the court room.

James packed up his briefcase, avoided eye contact with any of them, and left the building.

Healing Waters

With a lot of the building work at Healing Waters now complete, Kara had already moved in to prepare for her life as manager. For the past week, she'd lived in a bubble of contentment, decorating the little cottage on the property that was hers for the duration of her time there. She had deliberately avoided contact with her family during the legal saga with James, and was unaware of any developments.

She awoke that morning to find that Martin had left a bouquet of flowers and salted-caramel chocolate on the dining table.

"I don't do Valentine's Day, and…it's not even February. What are these for?" she asked, smiling with joy. Martin stopped her from speaking another word, and kissed her tenderly on the lips.

"This feels good, doesn't it? Us. Here?" He pulled back a little bit so he could see her face.

"It does, but I'm scared. Martin, people don't fall in love this quickly and move in straight way. What if we're making a mistake?" she asked.

"We're not other people. We're us. We've been hurt. We know what that looks like. And we know what this feels like. Stop fretting."

Most of the family had already gathered at Healing Waters to witness the bore drillers arrive. It was with great excitement that this land would generate its own income for forever and a day, due to its ongoing supply. Despite the anticipation and joy in everyone's hearts, the melancholic morning dragged itself slowly along the river's edge. While workmen were setting up, Eliza-May and Kara decided to finally get around to their girly chat, and headed up to the ridge. They had so much to catch up on, and the conversation covered many different topics. The mood was relaxed and easy, and it sure felt good to have a sister to chat to again. Each woman had expressed gratitude for being in Colorado, and although they had lived in various places they'd never expected to return here to live.

It wasn't Kara's plan to talk about William, but somehow that old wound was bubbling up to the surface. "I just don't understand how anyone can have an affair and break the sacred trust of those marriage bonds," she said, kicking the tufts of grass near her feet.

Eliza-May was reluctant to get into the rights and wrongs of monogamy and man-made or God-inflicted rules. Kara, having moved into the cottage, clearly hadn't heard about Clinton from anyone in the family.

"Sometimes things aren't always so straightforward," she offered.

"You think he was in the right?" Kara asked, confused.

"No, I didn't say that...it's just, sometimes life takes us in directions we never expected to go."

"But you'd never cheat on James, would you?" Kara asked, even though the idea was ludicrous.

"Kara, I don't love James anymore. I..."

"Yeah, but you still wouldn't cheat on him. I'm sure all marriages have their boring phases. You'll pass through it. He'll get over his tough lawyer shtick soon and you'll be one big happy family again. I mean, isn't that what all this legal rubbish is about? He just wants his family together. I understand the girls are happy where they are, and I'm not suggesting they should move back in, but I do get where he's coming from. This will all be over soon. A happy family. Honestly. Isn't that what you want too?"

"No, I don't want to be with him." Eliza-May turned to absorb the solemn sky. Perhaps Kara wasn't the person to speak with after all. She clearly hadn't heard anything from Azaria or Car about recent events.

Kara sat upon a large boulder. "So, what did you want to talk to me about? The other week, when I arrived at the health store, you said you needed to chat?"

Eliza-May didn't respond. Instead, she watched the fog rising from the river and thought about all the single mothers who would come to call this place their home, at least for a short time, anyway. "You'll be good here, as the manager. They've really landed on their feet as far as you're concerned."

"That's kind. Thank you. That means a lot." Kara smiled at her little sister, grateful they were going to spend more time together.

"You seem happy, too. Martin. He's good for you. I can see that. You're absolutely glowing. Radiant."

"I certainly didn't see him coming into my life, that's for sure. I guess good things come to those who wait," Kara mused.

"Maybe," Eliza-May sighed, her hands wrung together in frustration.

"What is it, Eliza-May? Just spit it out. I know something's bothering you."

She sighed, not knowing where to start. Kara would never understand. Not in a million years.

"I'm pregnant," Eliza-May said. There was no sentiment. No joy. It was just a statement of fact with as much passion as a weekly grocery list.

They were words that Kara had wanted to say for years. She'd imagined them so many times, and the joy she'd feel as new life grew in her belly. Words that meant she'd finally achieved her one true dream: to be a mother. And here was her little sister, trapped in an apparently loveless marriage, and saying it as if it was the worst fate that could be bestowed upon her.

"Wow," Kara said, her heart not quite with it. "That's another thing I didn't see coming. This family sure is full of surprises."

"James is the father."

Kara laughed at the ridiculous statement.

"Who else would it be?" she asked, frowning but still chuckling, and shaking her head.

"I would have liked it to have been Clinton's baby."

"That chap from the bookstore? You're having an affair? *You*? Is that what this fancy haircut is about?"

"I haven't had sex with him, but...that was the direction we were heading in...until this. Until..."

"Why on Earth would you still be having sex with James if you fancied someone else?"

"James forced himself on me. We hadn't made love in years. Years! And then he was on top of me...too heavy for me to push off. Once!" Eliza-May began to cry. "That's all it took. And now my life is ruined! Bloody ruined. All my dreams of a happy-ever-after are gone. And to make it worse, I'm going to have to move back in with James if I have any hope of him dropping the court case before we have to see the judge again."

Kara stood there, that sombre day, her mouth open wide in utter disbelief. "Do you have any idea how many women in this world long for a baby? A baby of their own to love, to hold, to cherish? Do you? And you're acting like you've got maggots in your trash can! I can't believe how blind you're being. It's selfish."

Eliza-May retaliated like a rattlesnake cornered against a boulder. "Yes, it's selfish! Too damn right. I lived my life in James's shadow, watching him build his dream, never having any joy in my days, stuck in a high-rise apartment and attending his boring work parties until I couldn't stand to leave our home at all. I was stuck in a living hell. Moving back here felt like being born again. Like I could breathe. What is so awful about wanting that for myself? I've found love with Clinton. I want to be with him. But I can hardly run into his arms while carrying another man's baby. I have two daughters who don't even live with me. Do you have any idea how lousy I feel as a mother? Any idea at all? Whatever way I turn, I lose. Don't you get that?"

Kara walked away. The situation was incomprehensible to her. Eliza-May was the good girl of the family. She turned back to look at her sister. "You *are* going to keep this baby, right?"

"Why are you asking?" Eliza-May frowned.

"Because, right now, nothing you do would surprise me. For goodness sake don't give it away like Astrid did. One gaping wound in this family is more than enough for us to handle."

It was some three hours later when a fountain of water sprayed out onto the land. Whoops of joy serenaded the workmen. Ruby ran around under the spray, her flaxen hair dripping with the pure waters arising from deep within Mother Earth. It was undeniably a day of celebration.

The Sun was shining now, and somehow everything about the day seemed brighter. Except for Eliza-May. At some point she had to tell both James and Clinton that she was pregnant. She excused herself from the celebrations at Healing Waters, and drove up to the Lafferty Homestead with one thing on her mind.

Knowing she'd be alone for some time, Eliza-May rummaged through the apothecary in Azaria's barn, desperately looking for herbs that would help eliminate the creature festering within in her womb. That James would leave sperm inside rankled every inch of her being.

She knew that her mother could help a woman abort a baby through herbal tinctures but highly doubted that Azaria would ever have done it. *There must be something here*, Eliza-May said, crying, exasperated. *Something for exceptional circumstances?*

After a hopeless hour, searching through glass jars and packages of roots, resins, barks and berries, she sat down while deciding her next move. An unfamiliar dampness between her legs distracted her. *Odd*, she thought.

The sight of bright red blood staining her fingers jolted Eliza-May back into the present moment. Was she miscarrying? She couldn't help but smiling. There was a God! Suddenly, feeling quite ill and cramping, she sat down again. There was only a bit of blood, she decided after investigating her panties. It was still possible to spot this early in a pregnancy. She closed her eyes in an attempt at prayer, desperately hoping for a solution. Maybe, if she miscarried, neither man would have to know. Feeling like she'd been unfaithful to Clinton, Eliza-May hadn't been able to look him in the eye. He was prepared to give her time to gather her thoughts and do what was best for her family, but each day apart felt like a year.

Making the bold decision to tell Clinton before James, she drove over to his house. Her heartbeat, rapid and ferocious, let her know that she was in fight-or-flight mode. But surely, if he loved her, he'd understand? Her greatest fear was not having Clinton in her life anymore.

As she drove into the tree-lined street, her heart almost pounded out of her chest. James was on the side of the road yelling at Clinton. What on Earth was going on? She wanted to turn away, to drive as far from here as possible, but it was too late. They'd both seen her.

Bracing herself for the confrontation, she bit her lip, then undid her seatbelt and slowly stepped out of the car. This ranked as one of the worst days of her life.

"Caught in the act," James spat out his words. "Slut!"

"That's enough. Don't talk to her like that. We haven't…we haven't even had sex."

"That's none of his business," Eliza-May said firmly. "James, I don't know what you're doing here but please leave Clinton out of this." Feeling queasy, she reached toward the trunk of a nearby tree for support.

"Eliza-May? What is it?" Clinton asked. "Honey, you're bleeding," he said softly, observing blood stains on her white jeans.

A spasm made her reach forward, and she moaned as the sensation ripped through her belly. "I think I'm… miscarrying."

"Slut!" James yelled, then turning to face Clinton said "So much for not having sex!"

Eliza-May fell to the ground, gripped by pain. "The baby is yours, James. Damn you!"

Clinton, ashen-grey, sat beside her. "Let me take you to the hospital. I'm not comfortable seeing you in pain like this. Come on, let's go." He ignored James's fury, and led Eliza-May towards her car.

James laughed, shaking his head in disgust. "Well it ain't my baby. We've not had sex for, oh, how many years is it now?"

He didn't remember.

"Of course you don't remember! You were so drunk you didn't hear me say 'no' to you over and over again." Eliza-May sobbed, Clinton's hands holding hers.

They drove away, not saying a word. Although it was only a five-minute journey to the hospital, it seemed more like an hour. The excruciatingly uncomfortable silence seemed impossible to break.

As Clinton pulled into the parking lot, his knuckles white against the leather steering wheel, he asked tenderly, but firmly: "Did James rape you?"

Eliza-May answered in the only way she could. She fell into his arms and said "I'm sorry. I'm so sorry. I didn't want..."

The doctor insisted Eliza-May stay overnight. He confirmed the truth: she had miscarried a baby. Grateful that the saga was finally over, she burst into tears with deep relief. But when the doctor smiled brightly and said there was a twin alive and well in the womb, she stopped crying and couldn't speak at all. For a few hours she'd been relieved at the possibility that the creature formed by James's evil sperm had perished within the walls of her womb. But now, like some never-ending nightmare, there was life, but not hope. Something, she didn't know what, had taken root right within the depths of her. Why couldn't it have been Clinton's baby? Everything would have been different then. They'd have raised the child together, with love, and had a joyous future to look forward to. But this? This was not good at all. Like a traumatised rabbit in headlights, Eliza-May was blinded by the truth: she would be inextricably tied to James Megane for the next 18-or-so years. Tears subsided, and in their place was a gnawing ache eating away at her. No matter which road her thoughts went down, they always seemed to arrive at a dead end.

Clinton didn't leave her side, and slept fitfully in a hard, plastic chair all night, listening to Eliza-May whimper softly, burdened by haunted slumber.

His first words, at break of day, were: "I'm not leaving you, Eliza-May. I can only begin to imagine how you feel. I'm here with you, honey. I'm always going to be by your side. Please don't let that man intimidate you anymore. I know you feel it's too soon for us to live together, but my door is open. I will not let him get in our way. Trust me, I'll do whatever it takes to protect our love. We can raise the baby together. You don't need James, and you certainly don't owe him anything. Don't give him the power to change your destiny any more than he already has."

A Light Goes On

A fragile blue sky bashfully welcomed Mahina to the old, abandoned lighthouse. She spent more than an hour slowly strolling around the land before taking the first brave steps indoors. Every moment was surreal. Even after all these years, her old home felt familiar and safe. This had been where she'd first learned about love, and what it meant to feel wanted. In the kitchen, she stopped abruptly as if instantly recognising something was different. Her measurement chart against the wall. And the words: *Your loving cousin, Starr.*

If she was honest with herself, she'd already grown to love Starr like she was a sister. So easy to be with, Starr's integrity and kindness were a healing balm for all the years Mahina spent without family. Oh how she wanted to meet her family of origin. Desperately. But there was one huge thing getting in the way: Anger. Mahina was so angry at her mother that she doubted she'd ever have anything kind to say. What sort of woman just gives away her baby? How could they possibly have any sort of relationship while Mahina had such rage constantly moving through her body? But she also knew Jenna Adams was right. She had to express how she felt, if for no other reason than that her singing career was dependent on her finding her voice again.

Torn between two worlds, she spent the next few days at the lighthouse, staring at the sea for hours, writing songs of love and longing, rehearsing what she'd say to Astrid. Running her fingers over Starr's name on the measurement chart for the hundredth time, Mahina knew the moment had come: She had to meet the rest of her family. And Astrid.

For five days, Eliza-May stayed off work. Isaac excused himself from the remaining building work at Healing Waters, and took over the running of the shop. He didn't ask questions, but trusted Clinton when he said she needed time off. He knew how much Eliza-May loved her job, so if she wasn't in a state to come in then there'd be a good reason for it.

Clinton lay beside Eliza-May, softly stroking her hair. She'd barely said a word since returning from the hospital. Her mind went in circles, working out the best possible solution. How could her new happy life unravel so quickly? If she moved back in with James, he'd drop the court case and that would spare her daughters any more upset. If she stayed here with Clinton, would she be slandered across town? And what of the unwelcome creature growing in her womb? She didn't want it. As much as she adored the two daughters that she'd created with James, this felt different. She was different. Clinton had promised to stand by her, and help raise the child as if it were his own. She cried at his generosity, but it wasn't enough. She had to find a way to get rid of it. There was nothing for it. She'd have to ask Azaria for help. It was that, or find an abortion clinic. Eliza-May sighed. She already knew that Azaria would refuse.

"Please tell me what you're thinking," Clinton begged.

"If I did," she whispered, "you wouldn't love me anymore."

"That's not true. It would never be true."

"I'm thinking that if I move back in with James, and put my daughters first, that I'd be doing the right thing."

Clinton turned away, valiantly blinking back his tears. "It's not what I want," he finally said, "but if you feel that is best, then I can't stop you. I don't have children. I don't know what it's like to have that level of commitment to a young person's welfare. I can imagine it, but I haven't experienced it. All I know is that I'd do anything for you, sweetheart, and if that means I have to let you go…" The tears refused to stay grounded, and he sobbed into her arms. "I love you, Eliza-May. Does that mean anything?"

For an hour or more, they cried together, desperate to never be apart, but also facing the inevitable: Eliza-May had no choice but to move in with James if she wanted to spare her children.

The next morning as Eliza-May opened her eyes, Clinton looked into them. Searchingly, desperately, hopefully.

"If he's raped you, Eliza-May, and I believe he has, then that needs to come up in court. Not only would the judge support the girls' current living arrangements, but James would be charged. He'd go to jail!" Clinton was firm, but kind.

"I don't want anyone knowing my business. I'm a private person. People would talk about me behind my back. I came to this town for a fresh start. I had years of being unhappy. I'm scared of going back to that awful place inside me," she said, pleading for him to understand.

"Keeping his evil deed a secret is more damaging. In the end, the only person's opinion that matters is yours. Not those of the townsfolk. Not James'. And not mine. Just yours."

"Clinton?"

"Yes, my love?" he said, touching her tear-stained cheek.

"Do you really want to be with me?" Eliza-May asked. "You'd be prepared to raise another man's child with me?"

"Don't ever doubt it for a second. I'm not going

anywhere. I love you."

"Okay. I'll do it. I'll tell James that I'm pressing charges."

Clinton kissed her gently on the forehead. "You won't regret this," he promised.

Eliza-May stood in James's office, and refused to take the seat he offered.

"You don't remember having sex with me. You were drunk. I begged you not to touch me, but you didn't listen. James, you raped me," she cried. Flustered, she continued: "You *forced* yourself inside me. I'm pressing charges."

"What are you talking about? Don't be so bloody stupid! You're my wife. All husbands get a bit drunk from time to time. It's my right to have sex with you."

"Is that what the law says?" she asked. "I'm carrying a child that I don't want all because you didn't listen! Do you have any idea what you've done to my life?"

"Your life? *Your* life!" He slammed the desk with his fist. "What about mine? I'm stuck in this town in the middle of nowhere, a man with no name, for Christ's sake, because I tried to support you! Do you have any idea what a failure my father thinks I am because I left New York? Do you?" Saliva spat from his angry mouth, and she felt its warmth on her cheek. It instantly turned cold.

"Go back. Go back to New York. You know the firm would take you back," Eliza-May said, hoping he'd follow her lead.

"What, so you can be with lover boy? No chance. If I can't have you I'm sure as hell going to make sure no other man can. Try pressing charges. No one will believe you, Eliza-May, not with your history of poor mental health. I'll just say you must have been having an 'episode'." He shuffled some papers on his desk, and asked "Is there anything else I can help you with?"

She wondered if she had ever really known him. Was he always like this? So mean, so controlling, so bullying?

"I'm going to the police to press charges." In a moment of self-assertiveness she said, "You won't have a leg to stand on if you think you're getting those girls back in your home. And you will never, ever control me again."

"Good luck!" he said as she left his office.

Once she'd gone from the building, he stood by the front door and watched to see where she was heading. Eliza-May was a pushover. He'd known that from the day he met her. Always more concerned with what other people thought than her own needs, James had been able to mould her into a subservient wife. Until she became nothing but a shadow afraid of itself.

He had to do a double-take when he saw her stand in front of the police station house a few hundred yards down the main street. Surely she was only bluffing? If she'd really meant it then she'd have walked straight into the building. James laughed.

Coward! The words were barely out of his mouth when she took the first step. Then the second. And the third. *No. No, she couldn't be. Would she really press charges?*

James saw his life flash before him. "Amanda, take your lunch break now," he said sternly to his receptionist. There were no clients in the waiting room. He needed time and space to think. "Now!" he yelled, his face red with rage.

"Yes, Mr Megane," she said, blinking back the sting

of her tears. He'd only ever been kind and courteous. She couldn't understand what she'd done wrong. Scuttling from the office, she ran down the street.

James paced the room. Then, returning to the reception area, bolted the front door and put up the 'closed' sign. He knew the law would not protect him if a jury found him guilty. He'd never be able to practise law again. How dare Eliza-May pull a stunt like this? Why was she trying to ruin his life? He was the father of her children, damn it!

Tony, I'll call Tony, he said out loud, wondering if New York's best attorney would be able to get him off such a humiliating charge. Tony did owe him a favour. A life-changing favour, in fact.

"Don't be stupid!" he said to himself, pacing the room, his breath sharp. "It's my word against hers. They'll never believe a depressive over a respectable man like me. Never!"

Try as he might, even James didn't believe his own words. Eliza-May was determined to destroy him. She was so different to the women he worked with in New York. She was the woman who couldn't get out of bed most days. Nowadays she managed a shop. He laughed at the irony. Now, she dressed beautifully and took great pride in her appearance. Everyone agreed Eliza-May looked as if she'd just stepped off a catwalk. Truth was, she simply wasn't that woman from New York anymore. She was bold. Definitely more confident. But more than that, she was loved. James knew that with Clinton standing by her side she'd be able to see this through. Even her daughters thought she deserved to be with him.

James was clear about one thing: he was not going to go to jail on a trumped-up rape charge. Slowly, he opened the bottom right-hand drawer of his desk. From underneath a pile of papers, he reached for a small pistol.

It had been a gift from his father when he passed the bar. "The world is full of crazy people, son," is what he'd said. "Don't ever let anyone get in your way."

Admiring the sheen, James held it in both hands. The cold steel against his skin, strangely comforting, enhanced the level of power coursing through his blood. No one could ever take this moment from him. He stood in front of the mirror, and looked himself up and down. He cut a fine figure, a respected man about town who was held in high regard. With his finger on the trigger, he held the gun to the side of his forehead.

"Oh Eliza-May, you silly, silly girl" James laughed.

For three hours, Eliza-May sat beneath the whirring sound of a ceiling fan as she confided to a female police officer that her husband had raped her. She found the noise strangely comforting. It had a familiar, recurring pattern, and the words came easily from her as she relived that evening.

"Mrs Megane, may I ask: has this ever happened before?" queried the young police officer who looked barely old enough to be out of school.

Eliza-May was quiet for several minutes, staring out the window at the cars driving by, and inwardly assessing her marriage, her sexual experiences, and her life.

"When I was young, when I was first married, and perhaps until maybe a year or two ago, I didn't know it was called rape. It's silly, I know that now. I...just thought of it as his right, you know, to have sex with me because I was his wife. I thought it was my duty."

"Have you ever said 'no' to him before when he's tried to have sex with you?"

"Yes."

"Once? Twice?"

"You mean a week?"

"I mean ever."

Eliza-May could smell Chinese takeaway food coming from the next room. She sighed, and let out a long, excruciating breath.

"At first, when we were first married, maybe half the times we had sex I had said 'no'. I think he just assumed I was being shy. Back then, he wasn't drunk. He was perfectly sober. This recent time, this time that caused the pregnancy, he was really drunk. After I had Ruby, I had severe postnatal depression, and sex became less frequent. To be honest, I think he was seeing someone at work. He was rarely home before one or two in the morning. It suited me just fine, as I already knew that I no longer wanted to be with him. But it was hard, you know? I had two daughters, no income of my own or savings, and felt all alone in the city."

When Eliza-May left the station, she felt oddly happy. Recognising that it was the first time she'd shared her sexual history with anyone, and the burden that had been removed from her mind, she smiled at how free she felt. The last thing she wanted was for James to experience court life as a defendant — it would completely demoralise him — but Eliza-May also knew that she no longer wanted to be a victim. The only person who had the power to change that, and to change the course of her life, was her.

"I've got a surprise for you," Clinton smiled, whisking Eliza-May away from the hiss of the coffee machine in his kitchen. She breathed in the scent of his skin, grateful to be in his arms. In his life.

"What is it?" she asked, knowing that their life together was really beginning.

He'd seemed so much lighter this afternoon knowing she'd reported James to the police. It was just a matter of time now. James would be charged, and this whole custody saga would be over.

"I've bought us a house. Our own home. A place we can make memories. It's over near Ploughman's Park. I know it means we'd have to commute to work every day, but that place has had such special memories for us. It's about two minutes walk from the park. There's plenty of room for your girls to stay over, too. I want to show it to you."

"You did all this while I was at the police station?"

"No," he laughed. "I bought it a few weeks ago. I have just been waiting for the right time to tell you."

When she didn't reply, he asked "Have I jumped the gun?"

"Oh no, not at all. It sounds perfect. I just can't believe you've done it, that's all."

"I believe in us, Eliza-May. I always have."

"So what are we waiting for? Let's go!"

The drive was quiet, but it was a peaceful and pleasant feeling. There'd be no more hiding. Their love was out in the open now. Free. *They* were free. And together, they'd get through the custody situation and rape charges, and they'd raise this baby. Of course, they had no idea what lengths James would go to for that child, if at all, but together they were a team. A strong team. This was the beginning of the rest of their lives, and they couldn't have been happier.

Everything about the house made Eliza-May clap with delight. It overlooked the river, and light streamed in through the vast windows. Built from Colorado pine, the house had a relaxed ambience throughout.

"Oh, this open-plan kitchen is gorgeous. All this light streaming in here. And look at those views over the river. How did you find this place?"

"Perfect timing, I guess." He pulled Eliza-May into his arms. "Marry me. Say you'll marry me. Say you'll spend the rest of your life with me, Eliza-May."

"Of course I will. There's nowhere else in this world I'd rather be. You've given me my life back. I love you, Clinton. Of course I'll marry you!"

And then, the moment they'd been longing for since they first met, became inevitable. Slowly, ever so slowly, Clinton removed her clothing.

"You are so beautiful," he said softly, his hand gently stroking the side of her face.

"Will you make love to me?" Eliza-May asked.

He nodded, and then removed his own clothes.

Eliza-May had never known such tenderness, and the sweet softness of each touch suggested that Clinton Hallett was going to be in her life for a long time. And with that promise, her body opened like a rose, quivering, beckoning him inside like a flower luring a bumblebee on a heady Summer's day. He eased himself inside, grateful to finally be home. They laughed, and cried, too, as their love showed them their bond was unbreakable.

A Light Goes Out

The whole town came to a standstill that bleak morning as the horse-drawn hearse pulled through the main street. Not a single shop was open. An eerie quiet said everything that the townsfolk were unable to say: a good man had died.

An icy wind tore between the shop buildings, determined to reveal the truth: sometimes life isn't fair.

Eliza-May was flanked by her entire family, her daughters sobbing uncontrollably at her side. Isaac, Bob, Martin, and three business owners carried the coffin on their shoulders and walked reverently into the heart of the woodland cemetery. This was a day no one saw coming, though for Azaria the words 'family reunion' now made perfect sense. She blinked back her tears as she watched her beautiful daughter and granddaughters frozen in time.

The graveside burial ceremony took thirty-five minutes, the words simple yet meaningful. Azaria observed her daughter standing there, no tears in her eyes. No outer signs of grief. She'd not spoken a word to anyone in days.

Isaac squeezed Azaria's hand. "We need to take her back to the homestead. She needs family around her."

"Isaac. I'm so scared. I don't know if she has the strength to get over this. She loved Clinton with all her heart."

Bob came over to Isaac. "Has James confessed to shooting him yet?"

"No. The police know it was him but he's remaining silent."

"Azaria, love, let's get your family home. All of

them. We need to be together right now." Isaac hugged Azaria tightly.

"I'm going to drive you home," Kara said tenderly, reaching for Eliza-May's hand.

Eliza-May nodded, the hint of a tear forming in the corner of one eye.

"I loved him, Kara. I really loved him." And then there was no stopping the avalanche. Eliza-May crumpled to the ground, despite the icy chill. "It hurts! I want him back."

"I know. I know you do. Come on, let's get you home." Kara reached down for Eliza-May's hand once again. "We've got you, honey. We've got you."

Martin came to her aid, and together they drove her slowly up the mountain. Home. Everyone was going home.

When they pulled up outside the Lafferty homestead, Eliza-May said "Can you wait here a minute, before we go in?"

"Sure. Of course we can," Kara said.

"There's something I need to ask you. You don't have to say yes. And you don't have to answer right now. But I do have to ask. It's all I can think about right now."

"What is it?" Kara asked, concerned for her sister.

"Will you raise this baby? Will you adopt it? And will you love it as your own? I can't do this. I can't go through this, but I don't want this child to leave a family that I know is filled with so much love. It belongs here, just not with me as the mother. I really can't do this."

Kara couldn't speak; she couldn't even think, but she could feel Martin squeezing her cold hand. They'd had many conversations about her desperation to have a child of her own, and how there'd been ample opportunities to adopt a child when she'd been at the orphanage, but something about it didn't feel quite right. It wasn't something she could ever put her finger on.

She'd spoken so unkindly to Eliza-May that day of the bore drilling, and the rift had been left wide open. Was this Eliza-May's way of saying she forgave Kara? That, more than anything, she needed her?

"Take as long as you want to think about it," Eliza-May said. The silence between them was excruciating.

"I feel honoured that you've asked me, but I don't know if that's enough. I don't know if I'm the right person, or this is the right circumstance. I will think about it. Thank you. But for now, the only thing I want to think about is how we help you get through the next few months. You've just been through such a horrible shock. Your girls are reeling that their dad has done this horrendous crime. We need to pull together. All of us. Come in and have a cup of tea."

Eliza-May walked ahead of them, greeted at the top of the veranda stairs by a long hug from Car, then Azaria, and the rest of the family. Most townsfolk were travelling up the mountain to join them for the wake. Car and Azaria had spent the previous day preparing food, and began to set it all out upon the table.

Martin looked at Kara and said "You can do this. You can raise that baby. I'll help you. How about it?"

Winter

Hope and Healing

For weeks, now, Eliza-May sat on the sofa in her mother's home, doing nothing in particular but looking out the window. The sweeping views across the valley and mountains were a constant salve to her weary eyes.

In many ways, the room was her pretty prison. There were no guards on duty, just attentive room-mates ensuring her basic needs were met. The living room looked as beautiful as ever: rustic, with massive wooden beams, and a cathedral ceiling which framed the expansive floor-to-ceiling triangle window. The great stone fireplace was a focal point, particularly at this time of the year as it framed the red and orange flames.

Isaac had stepped into Appleseeds and taken over Eliza-May's job. The toll of Clinton's death was impacting most of the family in one way or another. Azaria was at a loss as to how she could help her daughter. She wouldn't have described Eliza-May as depressed, but she certainly seemed unreachable. Occasionally she could get her to take a walk up to the beehives with her, but now the Winter winds were racing through the mountain, the weather became a good excuse to stay indoors. Car ensured that Eliza-May had regular meals, and fetched her tea by the half hour.

It was a bitterly cold Tuesday morning, and Car decided to do some knitting for the baby. She sat next to Eliza-May on the sofa, trying to make conversation, but rarely received any sort of answer. Azaria was in the barn tending to tinctures and making spicy mead. Astrid and Bob were now happily living down at Healing Waters, as were Kara and Martin, and only came to the homestead about once a week for a family meal. They were hoping to open the residential home in the early Spring. Starr had been hanging out in the barn, pen in hand, writing masses of notes for her syndication project, and enjoying her mother's company for as long as she could before returning to Australia.

Ruby was still her delightful self, able to make everyone around her laugh, but something had changed deep within her following her father's cruel act. Any day now he was due to appear in court. She asked countless questions, and never seemed to find the answer she so desperately needed: how could someone she loved do something so cruel?

Car looked out the window. "That looks like snow coming in. Weatherman said it's going to be a long Winter."

Eliza-May didn't reply, but when a knock came at the front door she looked up and asked "Who's that?"

"Can't say I'm expecting anyone," Car said, laying her knitting to one side. Her walk to the front door was slow and measured.

As she opened the door to the veranda, the vision before her was something she'd imagined for almost half of her life. But today? Today she hadn't actually given it a thought because she was so intent on being fully present for Eliza-May.

"Mahina. My beautiful granddaughter," Car cried, shaking her head in disbelief. She wouldn't have recognised her so quickly had she not known Mahina was a famous singer. "Please come inside. I can't tell you how long I have waited for this day. May I hug you?" Car asked, tears slipping down her face.

"Of course, of course you can." Mahina was overcome with emotion. She hadn't been expecting to feel this way, and it never occurred to her that the first person she'd meet here would be her grandmother: the woman who encouraged Mahina's cousins to pray for her each night.

They hugged for the longest time, both of them crying, until Car said "Get out of this cold wind. Come inside."

Starr had been in touch with Mahina and shared the news of Clinton's murder, and how it had rocked the whole family. She'd not had any reply and assumed it meant that Mahina had no interest in her family of origin.

"I heard the sad news," Mahina said softly. "I hope I'm not coming at a bad time, it's just that I'm conscious that Astrid is so unwell."

"Your timing is perfect, my dear. It's just me and Eliza-May here right now, but I'll call Astrid shortly."

Car led the way to the lounge room. Eliza-May looked up and smiled so brightly, and said, half laughing, "You came! This...oh this is the best news." She stood up and embraced her cousin. "Welcome home," Eliza-May said softly. "I can't tell you how good it is to have you here." In that moment, it was as if recent events hadn't happened at all. In some odd way, seeing Mahina transported her far enough into the future that Eliza-May was able to put a thick blanket between her pain and pleasure.

"I'm so sorry for your loss," Mahina cried. She was an emotional wreck. Despite every intention to be on guard, and keep her emotions intact, already she felt fragile and at sea.

"Thank you. It is taking a lot of getting used to. I'm," she looked over at Car, the enormity of her family's love finally hitting her, "I am just so lucky to be part of this family. There's no way I'd have survived without them."

Car excused herself to make them all tea, and Eliza-May and Mahina chatted some more, but it focused on the mundane: the wild Winter weather.

Car took the kettle from the top of the Aga and poured water into the teapot. She gathered some cookies from the cooling rack, and just as she was ready to leave the kitchen, she could see Starr and Azaria coming out of the barn. Her whole body filled with joy. Family. Beautiful family. She knew it was time to call Astrid, but she selfishly wanted a few more minutes with Mahina that weren't complicated with wounds of rejection and abandonment.

With the tray now on a small table beside them in the living room, Car looked up and smiled when Azaria and Starr walked into the room.

"Mahina!" Starr squealed. "You're here. Oh my God, I can't believe it. I mean, I knew you would, but... oh just come and give me a hug!" They laughed like old friends, so grateful for each other's familiarity. "This is my mom, your aunty Azaria," she said, introducing them.

"Such a pleasure to finally meet you," Azaria said. Each woman had tears in her eyes. "Astrid is going to be over the Moon. Ma, have you called her yet?" Azaria asked, looking at her mother curiously.

Car flushed a little, knowing full well that it should have been the first thing she did. "Just about to," she said, grinning at her daughter and heading to the phone.

Azaria hugged Mahina for a second time.

"This is just what this family needs right now," Eliza-May said. "Good news."

"Astrid still wants to meet me, then?" Mahina asked nervously.

"Without doubt," Azaria replied. "We all did, you know?"

The women settled down to lively conversation, and despite the icy snowflakes now falling outside the window, Azaria's heart melted like butter on a balmy day to see Eliza-May finally engaging fully with other people. The room was warm, and the fire flickered in celebration.

Car hadn't told Astrid that Mahina was here, she simply said to Bob "I think you and Astrid should come to the homestead without delay." She didn't need to say anything else. He knew exactly what she meant.

"But I thought we were going up to Azaria's tomorrow for dinner. Why are we going today?" Astrid asked, confused by Bob's sudden desire to head up the mountain.

"Yeah, we can still go up for dinner tomorrow, but it's good to do spontaneous visits, too. Especially with all that Eliza-May has been through. Never underestimate the power of a friendly face," he smiled. They made their ascent along the winding and bumpy dirt road.

"Whose car is that?" Astrid asked when they pulled up outside.

"Probably one of Car's knitting buddies."

Bob helped Astrid into her wheelchair, and then when they got to the steps, he held her securely as she made her way onto the veranda.

"Sure is cold. That snow might be settling, you know. We may end up needing to stay in the loft tonight," he said.

"Perhaps coming here spontaneously wasn't such a great idea?" she said.

When they entered the house, Astrid was struck by all the laughter coming from the living room. It almost sounded like a party. Bob pushed her in the wheelchair, his joy evident for all to see when they entered the room. Astrid took several seconds as she registered everyone's faces. And there was Mahina. Beautiful. Elegant. Smiling.

Mahina stood up, somewhat shocked to see how frail and vulnerable her mother looked.

"Astrid?" she asked nervously.

Oh how Astrid would have loved Mahina to call her Mom. But that was asking for way too much. Too soon. Not now. Not yet. But *when*?

She simply nodded her head. "Yes. Yes. I can't believe you're here."

"I just needed time. And I know time isn't your friend, and I'm sorry. I'm so sorry for that, but I just wasn't ready."

"Are you ready now?" Astrid asked, concerned that it still might not be the right time.

"As I'll ever be."

Car spoke up. "Why don't the rest of us go to the kitchen and leave Astrid and Mahina alone for a bit?"

Mahina looked alarmed. "No, it's fine. Really. All of you can stay."

Astrid's heart sank. Didn't her daughter want to be alone with her? Why had she come all this way if she was too scared to spend a few minutes together? She felt Bob's hand slide to her shoulder in silent support.

Car said, "Well, we need more tea and cookies. Azaria and Starr, come and help me. Eliza-May, you keep yourself warm. Bob, there are more blankets and cushions in the blanket box if needed."

Mahina sensed how upsetting Astrid found her need to have other people around them. She moved in closer, and dropped to her knees. "It's good to meet you, mother. It is." Her hand, ever so softly, reached for Astrid's cheek. She wanted to say 'I forgive you', but instead, used all her might not to say 'I'm so damn angry at you!'

Astrid's head dropped, and she sobbed. Until this moment she had no understanding of the potency of those words. Years of guilt and torment had torn through her body like bandits raiding a small town. Bullet holes in every conceivable place.

"Thank you," Astrid said between sobs.

"Let me make you comfortable," Bob said, putting some blankets onto Astrid's lap.

The afternoon whizzed by, and soon Ruby and Isaac arrived, followed by Bella, Callum and Chandra. Kara and Martin came later on in the evening.

Mahina was somewhat overwhelmed by all the new faces and names, though it didn't take long to really get a sense of how strong the family bonds were. But there was something nagging her that she couldn't quite put her finger on. She kept looking from Azaria to Astrid. Twins. The similarities were obvious, despite the differences between glowing health and debilitating illness, and their very different sense of dress. Azaria's hair, a silver crown of thick lustrous locks; and Astrid's bald head, with a few determined hairs growing in patches.

Mahina watched in admiration at the way Ruby snuggled in between Azaria and Isaac, determined to claim her space, and how little Chandra kept pulling at Azaria's hair with glee. And yet that undeniable sense of family, and the love that filled the room, disturbed Mahina. She'd wondered her whole life what it would be like to have this, and now it was hers. But, was it really? This was Azaria's family. Sure, Astrid was part of it, but all these children and grandchildren and great grandchild, they were Azaria's story. She was clearly a woman who loved hard and deep, and whose life was centred around caring for people.

And what of her mother, Astrid? Her family consisted of a daughter she gave away at birth as if she was from a litter of kittens and not necessary to requirements: something to hide in a hessian sack with a heavy stone, and drop in a pond without another thought.

Mahina watched as Azaria headed to the kitchen with the tray of empty mugs. That was her cue.

"I'll help you," Mahina offered, catching up with her. Conversation was easy, and they laughed a lot. In some ways, it was as if they'd always known each other. They lingered by the Aga, washing and drying plates and mugs, chatting about herbs and honey, laughing about Chandra's facial expressions when she gets excited, and about life on the mountain, when Azaria asked "How are you finding all this? It's a big family, isn't it?"

Mahina nodded.

"Are you okay? No regrets about coming here to meet us all?" Azaria asked, concerned by Mahina's silence.

"It's a great family, but it's not mine. It's yours. Azaria, why couldn't you have been my mother?"

Astrid's wheelchair came to a standstill at the doorway of the kitchen, and both women looked at her, alarmed at the words that had just been spoken. Words that could never be reclaimed.

If Mahina could take back the words she'd said, or at least have waited until she was certain no one but Azaria would ever hear them, she would. They were cruel words, but that had not been her intent. For her, it was just that Azaria made mothering look easy. She exuded love and happiness from every part of her being.

Astrid was frail and vulnerable, and showed no ability to care for anyone. Bob tended to her every wish. Astrid had no need to take care of anyone, not that she could have anyway, not with her state of illness.

They hadn't said more than a few polite words after the episode in the kitchen. It was obvious that Astrid was devastated, when she slowly wheeled herself back to the living room.

Azaria had simply replied: "It wasn't your destiny to have me as your mother, but I will do everything in my power to help you love Astrid. And to find a place in your heart where you can forgive her."

Isaac and Azaria crawled into bed late that night, shattered from another long day. It had been overwhelming, yet so incredible to have Mahina here at long last. As they began to make love, Isaac pulled away. "I'm so sorry," he said, angrily. It was the fifth time in about three weeks that he'd attempted to make love only to have his body let him down. His flaccid penis, now like a sea slug, nestled limp against the hair of his testicles. Out of commission. Redundant. Surplus to requirements.

"I'm just tired. All those hours I'm working at Appleseeds, then down to Healing Waters most nights to help Bob, well, I'm just tired."

"And…"

"What?" he asked.

"You're sure it's not me? Maybe you just don't find me attractive anymore? If I were younger, more toned, perhaps, then you'd rise to the occasion even if you were tired, surely?"

Isaac sat up and shook his head. "I already feel bad enough. Useless. The last thing I want is you thinking I don't find you attractive. It's simply not true. But I can't force myself to keep an erection. I'm sure once Eliza-May is back at work, and Healing Waters is complete, then things will return to normal in bed. Be patient with me, honey," he pleaded.

Intellectually, she knew he was right, but her heart

233

ached. Her greatest joy these days was their lovemaking, for it was one of the few times where she didn't tend to think of Luna. Lovemaking was a sanctuary from eternal grief. A blessed escape.

She kissed him goodnight, and then rolled onto her side, staring out the window, looking for traces of moonlight behind the snow-laden clouds. She heard him sigh. Isaac wanted to put his arms around her, and assure her that he still loved her, but he was held back by the old phrase: actions speak louder than words.

It was a nightmare Mahina had repeatedly had throughout her adult life: *the old janitor at the convent would lure her into the wardrobe with candy, and the promise that if she came inside he'd give her parents of her own. And for years, she went into the wardrobe, ate the sweet treats like she was told, and then...*

She awoke from the nightmare, crying and gasping for air. It was always the same. Always stopping at the same place, as if she knew she simply couldn't relive it. Her relationships had been few and far between, casual affairs that barely went beyond a couple of dates, and rarely resulted in sex. The few times that they did, she'd end up crying and running from the room. In the end, the trauma was too deep to keep reliving, and so she gave up on men and devoted all her time and energy to songwriting and performing. To her inner child, having sex meant one thing: she'd find her parents. The only thing was, it never did; she was always left feeling empty.

The next few days were challenging for Azaria, Astrid, and Mahina. The words could never be erased, and yet Azaria knew with all her heart that if Mahina just gave Astrid a chance, that they could forge a bond. She had hoped, at some point, that Mahina might go and spend time at Healing Waters rather than stay here at the homestead, but when Azaria broached the subject, Mahina said "no". "If I'm in your way here, let me know, and I'll go back home."

"You could never be in the way. My concern is that the relationship you and I are developing will get in the way of the one you need to build with Astrid."

"Car and I are going to Appleseeds with Isaac today, "Azaria said over breakfast. Isaac looked at her questioningly. *What is she up to?* he wondered, but went along with it.

"Would you like some help?" Eliza-May asked, which caused everyone around the farmhouse table to look at her in surprise.

"Mom. Oh Mom. That would be amazing!" Ruby raced around the table and hugged her mother. "I know we can't bring Clinton back, but he'd be so upset to see you sitting around here."

"He would, wouldn't he?" Eliza-May agreed. "I'm also thinking of going to the house. The house he bought for us. Would anyone like to come with me? It's really lovely."

"I will," Starr said immediately. "Do you have any plans for it?"

"Yes, I'm going to move in. That was his dream for us. He's not here, but I am. I need to find a way to move forward. Maybe moving in there; and then," she said, looking at Isaac for confirmation, "I could go back to Appleseeds and manage the shop?"

He nodded, and said "I'd be delighted."

"So, it's just going to be me and Mahina here today,

then? Bob's going to be working down at Healing Waters," Astrid said, alarmed that neither she nor Mahina would be able to hide behind other people and conversations. The moment of truth.

Starting Again

"I'm so proud of you Eliza-May," Starr said, reaching for her hand as they stood in the kitchen of Eliza-May's new home on that bitterly cold morning. "You are amazing. No one is expecting you to move forward or do anything you're not ready for. Honestly. There's no hurry, and there's no pressure. We're all just here for you. You know that, right?"

"Oh I do. I promise you I do. It's just been so comforting to sit at Mom's, in silence, and just feel my emotions. They've been turbulent, there's no question of that. But not once have I tried to suppress them or felt I needed to go on Prozac again. I felt heard and loved. What I've come to realise is that James never expected me to go into the police station that day. He thought I was bluffing. He wants me to fall to pieces. He expects me to spiral into depression. That's why he killed Clinton. It was the one thing he had control of. It's all so clear now, you know? And if I stop living my life, even though my heart has broken into a thousand pieces, it will be giving him exactly what he'd planned. James knew he wouldn't get away with this. He knows the system. Can you believe he'd rather spend years rotting in a jail cell than let me have a happy life with a new man? What sort of person does that?" she asked, still baffled by his cruelty.

"A control freak!" Starr added, bitterly. "A horrible man, quite frankly."

They toured the house, and Eliza-May chatted about her decorating plans for each room, including where her girls, and Chandra, could stay. Looking out the kitchen window, she described what the garden would look like if it weren't covered in a foot of snow.

"I've asked Kara if she'll adopt the baby, but she's not given me an answer yet," Eliza-May confided. "I'm getting nervous now. What if she says no? She's desperate to be a mother, and I know she'll be amazing."

"You're sure you want to do that? I can understand why you might not want to keep the baby—I do, I really do—but it would be growing up right in front of you and you'd have no rights; and no say, in how it was parented. Are you willing to give that up?" Starr asked.

"Kara is desperate to be a mother. I'm already one, and I don't want a baby with a man who…"

"A man who raped you?" Starr asked, finishing off the sentence.

Eliza-May nodded. "I know it seems stupid, given how wonderful Bella and Ruby are, and that James is their dad, but this one feels different. And I don't want a child of mine growing up with me always having that horrible memory to haunt me. It's not fair. But if it grew up with a mother who saw him or her through eyes which weren't tainted in any way, then he or she would have a fighting chance at an amazing life. I only want the best for the baby."

"I understand that. James appears in court tomorrow. Are you going?"

Eliza-May shook her head. "The whole town will be there. People want justice. Everyone's so angry, and clearly still in shock. Things like that don't happen here. Clinton was so well-loved and admired. I just don't know the answer. I want justice, don't get me wrong, it's just that James is Bella and Ruby's dad. I want him punished—he's a cold-blooded murderer—but what about James, the man who is their father? They're already so confused and distressed. It's so hard."

"Of course it is." Starr hugged her sister for the longest time.

"Nothing that happens to James actually makes anything better. Those girls have to live with the fact that their father is a murderer, and will they even want to visit him in jail?"

"Have they talked about this with you?" Starr asked.

Eliza-May shook her head. "So far, neither of them wants to see or have anything to do with James. But that will change at some point, even if it's just to get some answers or some closure. I'm not worried about Bella so much, but Ruby is so sensitive to everything. It's like someone stuck a knife in her heart. I think she's questioning who she is, as a person. We've not talked, but I can see it on her face. I want to talk about it with her, I really do, but...but I feel like it's my fault. If I hadn't fallen in love with Clinton, none of this would have happened." And then, she said: "I'm really looking forward to moving in here, and making myself a home. I need repair time. And that has nothing to do with Clinton dying. Being killed. It's to do with all the years I was trapped in that high-rise apartment. I'm still trying to discover what my needs are."

"Do you want the girls to come and live here with you?"

"No. I don't want that at all. I want to be on my own. Does that make me a bad mother?" Eliza-May asked.

Reluctantly, and somewhat against their will, Mahina and Astrid spent the day together at the Lafferty homestead. Mahina found herself making Astrid cups of tea, and ensured the fire was stoked well. They talked about different aspects of their lives, but every part of the conversation was stilted.

It took all her nerve, but eventually Mahina got the words up through her throat and out into the air. "I am so angry at you. Astrid, how could you give me up? I was a baby. Helpless. *I needed you.* How could you just think my feelings didn't matter? You didn't hold me. You didn't breastfeed me. You never rocked me to sleep, or patched a grazed knee. You never checked my homework or protected me from bullies. Not once have you soothed me after a nightmare. I know you're dying, and I hate the words coming out of my mouth, but they're the truth. You know why I said to Azaria that I wished she were my mother? Because she would have protected me!"

Astrid sobbed. What could she possibly say? Mahina was speaking the truth. Her words were like bullets straight into her heart: Astrid hadn't been there in any way for her daughter.

"Say something! Say something to make it better. Tell me I'm wrong. Tell me it broke your heart. Tell me you thought about me every single day. Tell me you regret it."

But Astrid couldn't find the words Mahina needed to hear so desperately. She didn't know how to love her daughter. Her sole motivation for finding Mahina was so she could be forgiven. But being a mother? Was that even possible? What would be the point when her days were numbered?

"I'm not Azaria. I never have been. I can't believe we are twins. We're so different. I just don't have her mothering gene. I'm...I'm selfish. I've always been like that. Everything is about me. That's the truth."

"So why am I here?"

"Because I want your forgiveness." Astrid confessed, searching into her daughter's eyes for redemption.

"And if I don't give it to you?"

240

"Then I shall die knowing that I got what I deserved," Astrid said resolutely.

"Don't you even want to try and be my mother?"

"Mahina, I don't know how!"

Nightmares

James's court hearing was scheduled for that day. He'd been silent all along, not pleading either way, even though the police had firm evidence. Car had written to him while he was held in custody begging him to plead guilty so that his daughters didn't have to endure a court case. She asked him to do this one last thing for Bella and Ruby: to show mercy for them in the way he hadn't with Clinton and Eliza-May. "Show me that somewhere inside of you still beats a human heart."

As on the day of Clinton's funeral, the whole town closed down. Justice would be served.

Eliza-May woke up early that morning, dressed in a beautiful lavender suit, put on her make-up, dabbed on the honeysuckle perfume Clinton had given her, and was just about to leave her beautiful new home. Turning the key in the door, she suddenly stopped and changed her mind. Instead, she went back into her bedroom and put on a pair of jeans, a thick jumper, and boots. She phoned Ruby and Bella and informed them that she wouldn't be going to court. She was clear about one thing: *she never wanted to see James Megane again.* They both asked if they could spend the day with her, and she agreed, saying that she was heading down by the river at Ploughman's Park for a walk.

"Dress up warm," she said.

Starr dropped Ruby off, and waited with her for Bella.

When she arrived at the park, Starr said "Hey, Bell, why don't I have some time with Chandra? You go with your Mom and sister. I'll meet you back at your Mom's house later. Okay?"

"Thanks aunty Starr. That's a great idea. I think she needs us today."

"I think you need her, too," Starr said, her voice cracking, and tears giving away her fragility.

Since Clinton's death, Starr had thought non-stop about Tobias, and how much she'd given up by coming back to America. Day after day, she fretted at how fleeting life was, and that at any given moment any of us could be snatched away by something out of our control. With an increasing urgency, she just wanted to fly back to Australia and resume their relationship. They spoke almost every day, but what she wanted more than anything was to spend whole days with him: to sleep against the sound of his heartbeat. But then, if she were over there, she'd be so far away from her family. And what if some other tragedy fell into their lives? Every day was a constant tug-of-war tearing her apart, confusing her about what she truly wanted from life.

Snowflakes drifted silently, that day of promised justice, landing unexpectedly on already-laden evergreen branches. The crisp air, and pale sunshine, ushered Eliza-May and her daughters, the three of them hand in hand, alongside the frozen river, where they walked for some time.

"When I met your father, I was a shy girl. I felt terrified of the world, but he was confident, and knew what he wanted in life. I don't think he ever really understood me, and that was probably the problem from the start, but I was taken in by that strength, and that is how I'd like you to remember him. As the man I fell for and chose to have children with, not that man who is appearing in court today."

"Have you forgiven him already, Mom?" Ruby

asked, quite surprised by her mother's tone.

"Already? I can't imagine ever forgiving him!"

"Quite right!" Bella said, kicking the icy ground. "He's a murderer. He's not my father. I don't ever want to see him again. I don't actually have any positive memories of him, and I certainly didn't know him in the way you describe him, Mom. He's a bully, and has been for years. That's why you became depressed. Don't you remember that? By being so ill, and stuck in bed; that was the only way you got out of under his thumb. Have you really forgotten how awful he was? The way he spoke down to you all the time. Well, I haven't forgotten!"

Eliza-May looked at Bella wondering if they were talking about the same person.

Ruby said, "I just remember that he was hardly ever home. Work always seemed more important. I want to forgive him. He made me. He's in me. I am who I am because I am part of him. I don't want to hate Dad. I want to understand what happened."

Ruby hugged her mother. "I'm so sorry your life has been difficult, and I know it's going to get better, but please don't be mad at me if I choose to visit him one day."

"That choice is yours, honey, in the same way that Bella can choose not to see him. I am the last person who is going to force anything on you."

Bella looked at her watch. Any minute now, court would open. She hoped her father just pleaded guilty and put everyone out of their misery.

Eliza-May's phone rang. Caller ID: Azaria.

"Mom? Aren't you in court?"

"There's...been a bit of a hiccup."

"What's wrong? Are you okay? Tell me. What is it?"

"James has escaped from protective custody. They

think he must have bribed the security-van drivers. The van was found abandoned, and there's no sign of the guards or James. I don't know what else to tell you, sweetheart. The courthouse was full. Everyone in town was there. There was barely standing room. People gathered outside on the pavement. We're all a bit speechless, really. The news stations are on overdrive."

"Do...you think he's going to look for me?" Eliza-May went from crimson to alabaster in seconds. Suddenly her beautiful new home didn't seem like such a safe refuge anymore. Would she be able to sleep alone not knowing where her murderous husband was?

"Isaac and I are coming home now. Do you want to meet us there?" Azaria asked, her tone filled with concern.

"Sure."

"Mom, you're scaring me. What is it? What's happened?" Bella begged.

"Your father has escaped. He's on the run."

"That's not good," Ruby said, "not good at all. Mom, promise me you'll stay with us at Gran's until he's caught?"

"I promise."

For four weeks, there was no sign of James Megane, and slowly everyone in the family got back to their routines and gentle way of life. After her explosive revelation of anger, Mahina spent most of her time with Astrid down at Healing Waters, getting to know her mother and trying to make amends for her cruel words. She doubted that she ever could.

But, each day, in little ways, they got to know each other, and often found themselves laughing at the same things. In the shower, just an hour after sunrise, Mahina surprised herself when she was able to sing a song right through, hitting all the low notes with perfection.

"When are you opening this place?" Mahina asked Astrid that morning, a couple of days before Christmas.

"I think we're just about ready. Kara has started with marketing, and putting word out to the appropriate agencies," Astrid said.

"What you're doing here is really wonderful. It's kind, and thoughtful."

"I know I ruined your life. I can't undo that. I'll never be the mother you needed me to be, but maybe in some small way this place will help other young mothers who find themselves in vulnerable or dangerous situations. I really do understand that it isn't a band-aid. I can't ever fully express how sorry I am, Mahina."

"Do you think that perhaps your body eating itself up is symbolic of all your guilt and regret?" Mahina asked courageously.

"It is certainly what I'm starting to think. My mother and sister believe so, that's for sure."

"Maybe instead of apologising to me, or waiting for me to forgive you, you could forgive yourself?" Mahina suggested.

It was an hour before sunrise, on Christmas Day morning, and Mahina was sitting in the kitchen at Healing Waters, sipping tea. Tears, fresh on her cheeks, spoke of another nightmare. If only they'd go away.

"Mahina, you're crying," Astrid said, when Bob wheeled her into the kitchen.

"Dust in my eyes."

"No it's not. You're crying. Whatever is the matter?

I thought…I thought things were better between us. Good, even. Have I said something wrong?" Astrid asked.

"It's not you."

"Would you like me to leave the room," Bob asked thoughtfully.

"There's no need," Mahina assured him. "It's just a recurring nightmare. It gets the better of me sometimes."

"What is it about?" he asked casually. Bob poured himself and Astrid a cup of rosehip tea, then spread jam on some sourdrough bread.

"You don't need to know about what goes on in my head in the dark of night," Mahina smiled weakly.

"Well, honey," he said kindly, "you're not just Astrid's daughter, you're mine too. And we'd like to know. Nightmares are generally things we haven't processed fully. I've got all the time in the world to hear about your monsters."

And it was that word—monsters—which kicked her in the guts and set the tears in motion again.

"There, there," Bob said, coming around to her side of the table and placing his arms around her shoulders. "We're here. Your mother and I. We're here for you. Okay? Talk to us."

When she stood up and hugged Bob, she finally knew what it was like to feel safe. Really safe. For a confusing moment—less than a sliver of a sublime second—she wished Bob was her husband, and not Astrid's. He was kind and loving, and she knew without doubt that he'd never hurt her.

"You really mean that?" Mahina asked, wiping her tears and blowing her nose.

"Of course we are," Astrid added. "Please don't doubt that. I may not have been there then, but I am here now."

Mahina took her time. It was a story so familiar to her, but one which had never left her lips. Her adoptive parents had an inkling, but had never heard Mahina's version of events. Mahina's story was about to come out into the world, and it was coming from her mouth, from her heart, from her torment.

"From the youngest age, maybe even before I could talk, I think, I was taken to a huge wardrobe in the convent most days. There was a word that I didn't know the meaning of, but it became the earliest word in my vocabulary: jurisdiction. The janitor said that I was 'under his jurisdiction', and that if I went into the wardrobe with him, I could have the five sweeties in his hand and he'd find my parents. He never did find me my parents," she said, blowing her nose again, "but each time I believed he would."

"Mahina, what happened in the wardrobe?" Bob asked kindly. "You can tell us."

She looked up at the ceiling, as if summoning a strength she'd never known existed might finally be possible, then took a sip of her cold tea. "At first, he'd just touch me between my legs."

Astrid gasped. "Honey, please don't say he 'just' touched you. That is more than bad enough. Evil."

Mahina continued: "At first he just touched me. In time, his hand went down my panties. I remember one time he pulled his finger out and there was blood on it. I just," she gulped back the tears. It was so hard telling the story, but Astrid and Bob were on the edges of their seats, willing her to go on. "I remember the smile on his face. As if it were a good thing, you know? But it didn't feel good. It hurt! It really didn't feel good. And I just wanted my mommy and daddy. He kept telling me to "shhh", and that he just needed to check something out. To check I'd been a good girl. He would keep putting his finger inside me, pushing it in deeply. I'd cry, and he'd tell me not to. He said if I stopped crying my mommy and daddy would be there soon."

Astrid couldn't bear it any more, but she knew that Mahina had to keep going.

"I am so sorry. I'm so sorry for every last bit of pain you went through. And more than anything, oh honey, I am sorry that your mommy never came for you. I understand now why you hate me so much. I really understand, and Mahina," Astrid sobbed. "I don't need your forgiveness. I most certainly don't deserve it."

Mahina stood up, and walked over to Astrid. "You weren't there for me. And you *never* came for me. But you weren't that man. You weren't responsible for his actions."

Bob said "Keep going, Mahina. If you want to." He clenched Astrid's hand as Mahina returned to her chair.

"It was my tenth birthday, and he said he had a special surprise."

"No," Astrid said, knowing what was coming next, but hoping against hope that she was wrong.

"I was ten. Ten years old. And that was the first time I had a man's penis inside me. It was a surprise alright, but it wasn't special. I vomited inside the wardrobe. He slapped my face, and brought me a cloth to clean it up. I hate birthdays. He said…that I had been a bad girl so my mommy wasn't going to come for me, but maybe another day, if I'd been good, she might. I know how ridiculous it sounds now that I'm saying this, as an adult, but when you're a frightened and vulnerable little child with no one in the world on your side, no one loving you, well you hang onto any sign of hope that you can. I really believed that one day my mommy and daddy would come and look for me. That they'd miss me and want to bring me home. The nuns said my parents were dead; but every day he took me to that wardrobe and told me the nuns were lying; and every day was another day when I went to bed crying because my mommy wasn't there. I know it might sound silly to you, but I don't have a wardrobe at home. I keep my clothes hanging on a rail without walls or doors."

"Doesn't sound silly at all," Bob said, tears trailing into his beard. He looked at Mahina, a vision of beauty despite her pain, and desperately wanted to protect her.

"How did it stop? What happened that you ended up with your adoptive parents?" he asked.

"That's the thing. One day, about two years later, I was bringing Mother Superior a cup of tea for one of the nuns, and she asked me how I was. It was the simplest of questions, but I said something like 'I don't know why, but I think the janitor is lying about my mommy and daddy coming to get me, and I don't think I should go in the wardrobe anymore', and she looked aghast. She asked me when I go to the wardrobe. I said it was when the nuns were praying in the chapel before lunch. She simply nodded her head, and thanked me for the tea. The next day, during prayer time, he was pushing himself inside me, prising my shaking legs apart, saying 'don't worry, pet, mommy will be here soon. Just wait a few minutes. Stop crying. Be a good girl', when Mother Superior opened the wardrobe. I don't know who was more shocked: him or her. She grabbed him by the hair and pulled him out of there. I'd never seen her angry before. She screamed and screamed, and threw a vase at his head. Mother ripped the rosary from around her neck and used it to tie his hands together. She told me to leave the room, and I never saw that man again. Ivan. His name was Ivan. And it seemed like only maybe a week or so later, that I was on a bus travelling a long way from the only home I'd known."

Bob nodded. "And this is the recurring nightmare?"

"It keeps stopping at the part where I'm waiting for my parents to arrive. And then I wake up with a start."

"Your parents are here now," Astrid said determinedly. "We're here. Bob and I are your parents. We are your family. I'm not Azaria. I'm never going to have her grace and flair at motherhood. I'm going to falter every step of the way, but I'll tell you this: I'm going to fight for you with every last breath I have, and I will never let anyone hurt you again. Especially me. I will never hurt you again. You have my word."

Springtime

The Promise of Hope

Eliza-May settled into her new home with ease, and loved to have her daughters over for dinner and the occasional overnight stay. Slowly, her heart adjusted to life without Clinton, but she knew without doubt he was nearby, loving her in an entirely new way. She felt his presence strongly in that home, and despite there being no sign of James being recaptured, she felt safe here. She had returned to work at Appleseeds, and thrived on implementing more changes into the shop. Isaac owned the vacant shops either side of the health store, and had plans to expand. Business was thriving, and it made sense to provide more. He made sure that Eliza-May was integral to the shop's future development.

The townsfolk rallied around, and Eliza-May felt herself wrapped in a blanket of community support. It was hard, she was the first to admit, to walk down the street and see the bookshop still with police tape across it: *crime scene, do not enter.* It wasn't so hard to see James's law business closed. She hoped at some point someone would rent the space and change the unspoken energy which lay dormant beyond the glass. It was a dark, stagnant space, but the memory of the man who was responsible for the town's pain left a mark no one felt strong enough to erase.

Ruby was standing outside the vacant barber's shop next to Appleseeds that sunny, Saturday morning, wiping the glass and peering in. Isaac was unpacking Azaria's herbs and honey from his truck in the street beside the shops. It was the fourth time in a month he'd seen Ruby looking

253

in that window.

"So, young lady, you still want to buy the old barber shop?" he chuckled, as he stepped onto the pavement.

"I do! It's perfect. I just don't know how to get the money, or how to get a lease in my name. But I will!" Ruby replied, determined to make her dreams come true.

"Well, Rubes, just so happens I bought that shop a while back. I'd planned to extend the health store and make a café on one side, and expand the fresh organic fruit and vegetables on the other side. We sell so much food in Appleseeds, it only makes sense."

Her face fell. "A café?"

"That was my intention. Why don't you tell me what your plans are? Better still, let me grab the keys and we can look inside."

"I can go in there?" she squealed with delight.

"Give me two minutes," he said, before ducking into the health store.

"Hey Isaac," Eliza-May smiled as he entered the shop.

"Just grabbing the keys for next door. Showing Ruby around."

"Is she still going on about having her little business there?" Eliza-May asked.

"Indeed," he laughed. "Indeed."

"You're not giving her false hope, are you?" Eliza-May asked, concerned.

"That's the furthest thing from my mind. Quite the opposite," he promised.

Ruby was tapping her fingers against the grimy window. "You've got the key?" she asked, her face lit up with joy.

"Don't get too excited," Isaac warned. It's really rundown in there. Needs loads of work."

"You do carpentry, though, Isaac. I'm sure you could help."

"Because I've got nothing else to do?" he chuckled.

"Well, Healing Waters is complete. And Mom is back at work. Azaria is really busy with the herb gardens. You need a little project." She smiled brightly, and Isaac just wanted to wrap his arms around her. Every so often he had to remind himself that she was Azaria's granddaughter, not his, though he did love her as if they were blood.

"Come inside," he said, thinking about her words: *you need a little project.*

"The thing is Rubes, I think it's probably bigger than that."

"You've got time, and I can't really run a business yet for a year or so, but I think we could start now."

"So, you want me to give up my café dream and let you have this for selling flowers?"

"I've already told you, it's not for selling flowers. Weren't you listening?"

He felt chided. Of course he'd been listening. She wanted to do flower readings for people. He just had no idea how someone so young, albeit intuitive, and, he had to admit, psychic, was going to market such a thing.

"I love what your plans are; it's just that I'm not sure you need a shop for it. Isn't it something you could do up at the land? Couldn't Azaria convert part of the barn as a space for readings? Or the loft?"

"Well, yes, but I keep being drawn to this shop," she said, sneezing three times in a row, as their movements stirred up the dust. "I don't want to be hiding behind closed doors. I want that glass door cleaned, and to be left open, the breeze coming in and blowing through my hair," she said, raking her fingers through the silky flaxen hair to emphasise her point. "I'll put a table over in that corner, and do my readings there. Over at this wall, I'll have steel buckets with blooms of every sort. When people want a reading they'll pick the flowers they want, and bring them to me."

"So, I guess I won't be opening a café in this shop then?"

Ruby jumped up and down, and gave him a huge hug. "You won't regret it, Isaac. I promise you."

"What do we do in the meantime with a vacant shop?" he asked.

"Get it ready of course! How about I meet you here after school each day and we can spend an hour or two just slowly getting it ready?"

"You've really thought this through Ruby Megane, haven't you?"

"Yeah, I have. One more thing. I'm changing my surname."

"Because of your dad?"

Kara had finally agreed that, yes, she would be over the Moon if she could adopt Eliza-May's baby. It made perfect sense. They decided to find a lawyer and get the appropriate papers drawn up. Eliza-May loved the skip in her sister's step, and knew without doubt it was the best decision. Each day she ensured that she exercised and ate nutritionally rich foods so that the baby could grow to be as healthy as possible.

Kara could still manage the day-to-day running of Healing Waters, and would wear the baby in a sling. Given the residential home was for mothers and babies, Kara could model a gentle way of parenting and lead by example. She would pass on the parenting skills she'd learnt from her mother, about having a huge family bed and sharing sleep. Baby would be worn throughout the day, and there'd be ongoing snuggles, and kisses and laughter. Her biggest challenge was how to feed the child. It deserved its mother's milk, but if Kara was going to mother the child from the start, then how long could she possibly ask Eliza-May to express for?

"You know, in India women who haven't had babies learn how to lactate so they can feed the orphans," Car said to her one day when the conversation of baby feeding came up. "I saw it with my own eyes," she said. "If you're interested, Azaria can make up some special herb teas to help stimulate a milk supply, and you could talk to Alison at Le Leche League about inducing lactation. I believe she's helped several women to do this."

"Actually, Gran, you know, I've seen this happen in Zululand as well. It's quite extraordinary, really, to see a woman who has never breastfed, spontaneously make milk. Not sure I can do that, but I'll certainly give it a go."

Later that day, side by side with Azaria in her apothecary, they gathered together various dried herbs: fenugreek, goat's rue, fennel, red-raspberry leaf, starflower, nettle, and blessed thistle. Azaria marked the packages: Mother's Milk Made With Love.

"You can do this, Kara. You really can," she affirmed. "I am so glad that baby is staying in the family. I couldn't bear another Mahina story."

"It's different these days, though, isn't it Mom? More open? Less behind closed doors?"

"Yes, it is, but have you and Eliza-May spoken about what you're going to tell this child? About who she is?"

"Yes, we're going to say that Eliza-May carried her in her belly, and I am her mother. And the rest, we'll just figure out as we go along. I know there are going to be bumps. And questions. Lots of damn questions. But I feel strong. It feels right, you know. And Martin is an absolute rock. We've got this."

Kara and Martin spent Saturday afternoons looking through shops, and finding baby clothes. Although Martin had raised two sons as a single father, he found himself just as excited about the impending birth as if it were the first time. They agreed on a name: Lucy Hope. Now it was just a matter of waiting. They spent more time with Eliza-May, hanging out and giving her support: Reminding her how much they were going to love this baby. All the legal paperwork was finalised.

The main focus for now, though, was putting preparations in place for opening Healing Waters. Kara sat at the table with Astrid and Bob, going through her marketing plan one more time. Spring water, bottled from the land, would soon be in production. To everyone's surprise, Martin chose to leave his new job, and become part of the Healing Waters staff. It made sense. He could always be on hand to watch a small team of people bottling water, and be nearby for Kara and little Lucy.

Mahina was in the kitchen, preparing lunch for them all, when she said: "I've been here these past few months, and I've not contributed in any way. Sure, I've bought food, but I haven't done anything meaningful," she said.

"Just being here is meaningful," Astrid insisted.

"Yes, but I want to do something. Something that... Mom, I want to do something that shows I've come to love you."

There was silence across the kitchen that Spring day. It took all of them by surprise, but perhaps no one more that Mahina. She ran the words through her head: *I love you.*

"Did you just call me Mom?" Astrid asked.

"Yeah," Bob said, "and she just said she loved you."

"Let me do a concert here. A benefit concert. A concert would raise enough money for this place to be financially secure for a good year or two even though you've got the bottled-water business. Please let me do that."

"You have just given me the greatest gift of all. Does…calling me Mom mean you forgive me?" Astrid asked nervously.

Mahina nodded.

Astrid stood up from her wheelchair, her legs wobbly and her arms shaking. "Come here my child. Come here."

They hugged, and laughed, and cried for quite some time.

"When?" Astrid asked, "When did you change your mind about me? What did I do? How did you forgive me?"

Sitting down around the table, Mahina reached for Kara's hand.

"Watching my cousin take on her sister's baby, and observing Eliza-May's torment. I can see that she wants the best for that baby, and is doing what she feels is right. But Eliza-May is a grown woman who already has daughters. I do believe she knows what she is doing. You were a girl. You were young and frightened and traumatised. No matter what you were feeling about me when I was a baby, I believe—well, I have come to believe—that you acted from a place of mothering instinct. You may have thought you didn't want me, or didn't love me, but I think you did. I think you made a decision to close your heart down to me because you were acting in my best interests. Obviously if you knew how my childhood panned out, you probably would have made a different choice."

"There is no question of that. Don't for a single

second doubt that. Ever."

"I know, Mom."

Astrid loved the word. She loved hearing her daughter say it, over and over again. She'd never tire of it, and for the first time truly understood how Azaria became such an amazing mother. It was the constant give and flow of love between mother and child that enabled the bond to become solid.

Astrid felt herself come alive with a joy she hadn't felt since meeting Bob, but this, here today with her daughter, surpassed any experience of her life.

"Mahina, I love you too. I truly do. I hope we haven't left this too late," she whispered, the reality of the future closing in before her.

"It's never too late to love."

Kara, Bob and Martin wiped their eyes.

"So, let's set a date!" Mahina said.

Kara opened the diary. "How much time do you need to prepare?"

"Let me make some calls. I will see when my band is free, and fly them over here. I'll need a makeshift stage, but I reckon we can use that front flower meadow by the river. We'll have to put up marquees and it would be a good idea to have refreshments of some sort. Any CDs I sell, along with the concert tickets, will all go to your home. Here. For the mothers."

Astrid kept nodding her head. Words were pointless now. They had crossed the great divide.

Ruby spent several hours immersed in reading the flowers. Luna, as ever, was right there talking to her.

"I want to know about Dad. Where is he? Why did he kill Clinton? Will I ever see him again? Do I have that evilness in me?"

"Too many questions, Ruby. You need to focus on your life. You have so much to give other people. You are in the world for a reason, and you're going to touch thousands of lives. You and your flowers! But for now, just keep doing what you're doing. The shop will be amazing. You'll love working with Isaac. He's a special man. Ma got lucky there!"

"Yeah, but Dad?"

"Ruby, darling, you have a special gift. But this gift isn't for you. It's for other people. You're a conduit," Luna said softly.

"Did he hurt those men? The men who were meant to take him to the courthouse?"

"Ruby, I'm going to say it once more: your work, your readings, they aren't for you, sweetheart."

Azaria, Isaac, and Ruby manned the refreshments tent, and were so grateful they'd recruited dozens of women from the town. Ten thousand people had booked tickets for the concert, and it sold out in hours, no small thanks to Starr's excellent publicity efforts across all social media.

Astrid and Bob stood in awe. All those bodies on their property. It was buzzing. This place was now their home, and the love of her family meant that it would be a beautiful home for many mothers and children long into the future. They spread out a picnic blanket as close to the stage as possible. Every band member had dropped what they were doing to support Mahina. All she said was that it was important. They didn't need to know anything else.

As the cello began, a soulful sound came from deep within Mahina's belly. The people in the audience looked around at the unfamiliar tune. Nobody knew the song, but by the end of it every single person was crying. Except for Mahina. She knew that song inside out. The band members had already rehearsed it several times, but even they were moved.

Mahina, known around the world for not speaking on stage, and never giving interviews, stood quietly for a moment before summoning up the courage to speak.

"Thank you so much for coming here today. It means an awful lot to me. That song I just sang was for my mother. Astrid, could you please come up here?"

Bob helped Astrid into the wheelchair, and then pushed it up the ramp. The sunshine warmed her skin, as the wheels took her across the stage. Astrid felt like she was flying.

"This is my mother," Mahina said proudly, introducing her to thousands of fans. "She's not well, and I wonder if you would all take a moment to join me in prayer and surround her in love. I don't know about you, but there's something I learned recently: it's that when someone sends you a kind thought it can really make a difference," Mahina said, smiling at Starr, a silent thank you for a thousand prayers sent her way in childhood.

"Thank you. All the songs I write, and all the things you love about my music, well they couldn't have happened if it weren't for my mother. My only regret is that I couldn't have had one without the other. I love my music. I love my fans. I love my life." She stopped, then, and looked into Astrid's eyes. "But I'd have swapped all of them for a day of my childhood with you. I love you, Mom. You were the right mother for me." She nodded to Bob, and he wheeled an overwhelmed Astrid off the stage. Did her daughter just publicly introduce her? Were they finally a mother and daughter to the world, and not some horrible family secret that had to stay hidden?

And the next song, one that everyone knew, had

people standing on their feet in ovation before she'd finished the first line.

Azaria was sobbing in Isaac's arms. "I never thought this day would come. It's a miracle."

"All of life is a miracle, sweetheart. All of it. Every single day. It's certainly a lesson in never taking anything for granted."

For four solid hours, Mahina performed to an enraptured audience, though she only had eyes for her mother. Tomorrow she'd have to let her down gently. She'd be returning to Nashville next week to get back to reality.

"You know, if James Megane were around he'd be huffing and puffing and telling me to study for a proper job," Ruby said to Isaac matter of factly as they moved some dusty shelves from the inside of the old barber's shop to the back patio.

"James Megane? You don't call him Dad anymore?"

"Dad doesn't feel right, you know? Can I tell you something, Isaac?"

"Anything, Rubes. You should know that by now."

"I feel really free without him around. It was like I was never good enough. Now I feel like I can do anything. That I'm in charge of my life. I feel strong. And really, really alive. It's a bit scary, but boy it feels fun, too! And, one other thing: You've always felt more like a father to me than he ever did."

"Ruby, that's one of the most beautiful things anyone has ever said to me. Thank you. I wish you had been my daughter, because not a day goes by where I'm not counting my blessings for you in our lives. You're an incredible young woman. I hope I'm around for many, many years so I have the pleasure of watching what you do with your life."

She pecked him on the cheek, and moved some other rubbish from the shop.

"Oh yes, and I have chosen my new name. I'm going to change it by deed poll, though I haven't told Mom or Azaria yet."

"Let me guess: Ruby Radiance?"

Ruby stopped in her tracks, her face suddenly white. "Oh My God! Are you psychic, too, Isaac? Please tell me you are. Tell me you know what this feels like, always hearing voices and seeing images."

"Sorry to disappoint you sweetheart, but you've been writing the word radiance everywhere: on your school books, in chalk on the veranda, you scratched it into the lovers' tree. It's even on the window in the car from when it had steamed up the other day."

"Oh," she said, disappointed. And then Ruby was back, her face brighter than the Sun itself. "So what do you think? Does it work?"

"It's pretty perfect, actually. Ruby Radiance, indeed!"

She hugged him, and then said "Come on, Isaac, we've got lots of work to do."

He hadn't the heart to tell her he was exhausted, and really just wanted to go home and get a few hours sleep. They carried on for another hour, when Ruby caught sight of her mother at the doorway.

"Mom? You don't look very well. Are you okay?"

"The baby. I haven't felt the baby kick all day."

"It might just be in a different position," Isaac said, trying to reassure her.

"The baby's gone," Luna whispered into Ruby's ear.

"No," Ruby cried. "No!"

It was a long night around the kitchen table at the Lafferty homestead that evening. A painfully long night. Eliza-May and Kara consoled each other, but it did little to ease their pain. Eliza-May was shocked by how much the baby she didn't want had impacted her, and how she would do anything in the world right now to have that little life back. So close, and yet so far. Maybe it was a blessing? Maybe that child would grow up with too many wounds? But what of the wounds here, now? Kara cried into Martin's arms for the longest time. The baby she'd always dreamed about — stolen — taken by an unkind god before she even got to kiss its cheeks.

As Mahina observed her cousins, everything became perfectly clear: this family needed her as much as she needed them. There was only one reason to return to Nashville: to sell her house, pack up her belongings, and bring Carnell here—home—to her family.

"Why?" Kara kept asking over and over. "Why has this happened? Mom, it's not fair. Why would this baby die? Didn't she know how much Martin and I would love her?"

Azaria shook her head. She was the last person to have any answers. She was still asking 'why did Luna have to die?' It was a question she asked on a daily basis.

Luna whispered in Ruby's ear: "Lucy came to bring healing. She helped Mahina see Astrid differently."

"I can't say that!" Ruby said out loud. Ruby's conversations with Luna were common knowledge now within the family, but she certainly kept most of them to herself. Isaac was her one constant confidante, but she wasn't sure she'd even tell him this.

"Rubes?" he asked, knowing exactly what was going on in that tormented little head of hers. "You know you can say anything. What you hear is safe with us."

"It doesn't feel safe. It makes sense, but it doesn't

feel like it would bring comfort."

"Okay." Isaac wasn't prepared to push the issue.

"Please tell me Ruby," Kara begged. "I need something to hold onto. Something to help me understand."

Ruby looked at Azaria, then at Astrid and Mahina.

She dropped her face into her hands, her flaxen hair falling all around her. Never had she felt the weight of this gift so heavily.

"Don't shoot the messenger!" she said cautiously. "I'm just repeating what Luna told me. I didn't make it up, I swear."

"We believe you, Ruby. We trust you." Kara urged her to continue.

"Luna said that the baby — Lucy — came to bring light into our lives."

"Lucy means light," Kara said, "But I don't know what you mean."

"She came to help Mahina and Astrid remember who they are. To help them see the light in each other."

Kara stood up, shaking her head, and walking away. "But...she was *my* baby!"

Turning The Page

Bella ambled along the main street with Chandra; the baby comfy in a stretchy sling, happily riding on her mother's hip. Bella kept looking at her watch. Two hours until Callum finished his shift as a lifeguard at the local swimming pool. This was always the toughest time of day, keeping Chandra happy until she saw her 'dada'. The morning always flew by, as Bella did her housecleaning, followed by a walk, and then back home for Chandra's nap. Usually, she'd pop downstairs into Appleseeds and visit with her mother for a bit, and they'd share lunch. But today Eliza-May was busy stocktaking and didn't have time to chat for long. Chandra was unsettled, so Bella headed off into town.

She'd long stopped walking by the river unless she had Callum with her. It had been hard giving up her friendship with Ivy, and many times she wondered if there might have been another way. Life had felt tough since her father killed Clinton, and she wanted a friend to talk to. She had Callum, and he was wonderful, but she wanted a girlfriend to share the story of her life. This little town meant the world to her, and there was nowhere she'd rather be. Everything in her life felt settled, and she'd even come to terms with her father's horrid act, but if there was one thing she wanted right now, more than anything, it was to have a friend. Somehow it seemed like Fate just wasn't prepared to give her that. It felt lonely being a teenage mom, even though she had a fantastic partner in Callum.

Standing outside A Novel Idea, Bella peered through the windows. Thousands of books, sitting on shelves, all with stories to tell. Her mother's pain, and the sheer devastation which swept through this mountainside town, had Bella wondering what was to become of the bookstore. It had been such a hub for the community, drawing book lovers from near and far. There wasn't another bookshop for thirty miles.

It was the reflection in the window which made her jump with a start.

She turned around. "Ivy! You scared me."

"I'm sorry. Bella, can we be friends? I have missed you, and our long chats by the river. I was only trying to help."

"No, Ivy. Not at all. I wish you well, but there is no room in my life for people who are cruel. I only want kind people in my world. And your words and your intentions were anything but kind. Please leave me alone."

"We're leaving town today, and moving on. I'd love you to come with us. You'd really fit in. Please say you'll come with us. God will forgive you."

"Will he forgive my father?"

"Oh no, not at all."

As Azaria crawled into her cosy and comfortable bed that night, she watched Isaac undressing. His taut muscles aroused her without any effort on his part. She adored the look of him, and often found herself weak at the knees. And that was when he had his clothes on! Here now, naked, she found herself tormented. It had been months since they'd made love. They'd loved each other in a thousand other ways, of course: the smiles they shared, and walks through the orchard and wildflower meadows, and the comfortable way they lay against each other on the sofa each night as Car strummed the guitar. In every other way they lived like young lovers, filled with pure delight in the other. Love was expressed in every little act of kindness and devotion, but right now Azaria wanted Isaac inside her. But she knew better. Every attempt had left them both disappointed. She wondered, though, was it going to be like this for the rest of their lives? It was cruel, to say the least. A love so strong, so defiant against the tragedies of life, and yet as vulnerable to human emotion and exhaustion as anyone else. She kept her thoughts to herself, and instead took a few moments to write her 'daily five' in her gratitude journal. By the flickering light of several beeswax candles, Azaria wrote:

1.) I am grateful that Eliza-May and Kara's relationship is stronger than ever. Their shared grief has bonded them in ways I could never have predicted. They both mourn the loss of their baby. I saw them walking hand in hand through the labyrinth this morning. I'm not ashamed to say it made me cry.

2.) Ruby's passion for her flower shop, not to mention the pride with which she wears her new name, puts a smile on my face every day. I feel her desperately itchy feet determined to open up that shop. But Isaac and I are adamant that she must graduate school first. I am so grateful for how much time and energy he has put into creating a beautiful space for her. He's like her personal guardian angel, attending to her every beck and call. I have to admit the place does look pretty gorgeous. All the locals are curious, and wondering when it will be open. I haven't the heart to say: in a couple of years! I did put my foot down about getting a signwriter in. "There is no shop name going over that window until you're ready to open." In that moment Ruby acted more like a defiant toddler than the blossoming young woman that she is.

3.) I'm grateful for Car's ongoing love. She's such a rock for us all, but in the most subtle and gentle of ways. It's easy to not even notice her in the room sometimes, yet I'm always aware she's there. She's not a woman to waste words. I love that about her. If there's one thing that gives me comfort, I know she'll be around for a long time. This family has seen way too much of death.

4.) So grateful for the abundance of blue flax blossoms in the garden this year. It's astonishing, and makes me smile every time I step off the veranda. I treasure this beautiful life. I am so grateful for my wonderful home and loving family. How did I get so lucky?

5.) Mahina amazes me. She's an incredible woman in her own right. A dandelion of this world who survived the odds and blossomed. But as I watch her, living nearby at Healing Waters, she continues to bloom. She is living proof that we're never too old to need our mother. Never.

Azaria sighed as she put her journal down. So much to be thankful for. Truth was she could probably write down twenty things each night, even on the worst of days.

"Good night, darling," Azaria whispered as she snuggled under the covers.

"Where are you going?" Isaac asked.

"To sleep," she said, as his arms came around her. Was he going to attempt lovemaking? Surely not? Why ruin a perfectly good day by doing something he knew would leave them both upset. Again.

"Isaac," she pleaded. "Don't do this to yourself. Or to me."

He kissed her gently at first, tasting her, remembering how much he lived for the feel of her skin on his. Azaria resisted, hesitant, and not wanting to be lured down a road towards heartache and inadequacy. She had never, not once in her life, felt bad about her body or femininity, but these past few months had left her questioning her validity as a desirable woman. But damn that kiss! He tasted so good. She wanted more of him, and had no choice but to respond. Her head told her 'no', but her heart and her body had no ability to refrain. A moan left her lips, an acknowledgement of a desire so raw and primal that she had to follow her urges.

"Did you like that?" he asked gently, kissing her bare shoulder, then her breast. She was already aroused. Her raspberry red nipples, firm with pleasure, beckoned his lips. Nuzzled against her chest, his week-old silver-butterscotch stubble gently abrasive against her ample breasts, Isaac said: "I am going to make love to you tonight, Azaria. Is that okay with you?"

She laughed. "You have to ask?"

"Always. I would always ask." His kisses, like mini torchlights, lit up ever inch of her body. The urge to become one with him drove her crazy, and her hips rhythmically rose up towards him, begging him to join with her. Teasing, yet promising with every kiss and thoughtful touch, that he was wanting exactly the same thing, Isaac took his time. They had months of making up to do, and if there was one thing he was sure of: tonight would be perfect.

"You are my life, Azaria. You're everything to me. I wish your life was easier, without the trauma and upset, but it is what it is. The only certainty is our love for each other, and the home life we've made together. I want you to marry me. I know it's just a bit of paper, but I want to say in front of our friends and family that you are the only one for me."

"Not sure where you're going with this, Isaac, but I have already said yes, so you don't need to propose again."

"But you do need to set a date," he said, his mouth now tantalisingly close to the apex between her legs.

"Oh," she moaned, "oh, don't stop!"

He rested his chin on his hands, leaning back on his elbows, and smiled. "You really look more incredible than ever from this angle," he groaned, her face in the distance glowing in the candlelight, and before him, her silver hair, like angel hair, crowning her doorway to heaven. His heaven.

"Have you forgotten what to do? Because, you know, I'm at exploding point."

He'd already figured that out for himself. Her moans of ecstasy were sure to have Ruby Radiance running into the room any minute. Isaac gave thanks for the headphones and music player he'd bought her recently. In this moment, he hoped like hell Ruby was plugged in.

With a gentle parting of her toned legs, Isaac came forward on top of Azaria, kissing her lips, and stroking her cheeks, his fingers combing through her long silver hair. He allowed her to guide him inside her, and the intensity overwhelmed them both.

"I want this night to last forever," she whispered.

Plunging deep into her molten core, they both moaned at what they'd been missing all this time. "Feels good, doesn't it?" Isaac asked, watching the smile on her face. He loved her fully that night, causing both of them to reach the stars, and then some.

"Mom, who owns A Novel Idea?" Bella's question came completely out of the blue, and caused Eliza-May to sit down. They were in the dedicated book area of Appleseeds, where she'd been sorting new books on health-related issues.

"Why are you asking me that?" Eliza-May asked.

"I'm sorry. I know it's raw for you, but I just

wondered if you knew, since Clinton was an only child and didn't have children of his own."

Eliza-May let out a long breath. "He owned the building outright. It wasn't a lease. He'd actually put it in both of our names when he bought the house. I think he said it was easier for accounting purposes or something."

"*You* own the bookshop?" Bella asked, shaking her head. "Why didn't you say anything?"

"What's there to say? I work here. I love Appleseeds. I love books too, but I don't think I want to run a bookshop."

"It can't stay closed, though. At some point you have to make a decision, Mom. It's just a thought…a random thought, and I'd need to check with Callum, but how would you feel about us opening it up again and running it for you? You know what that shop meant to this town. And at the risk of sounding like Gran, it would bring healing to this place."

"And to me," Eliza-May said, nodding in agreement.

Crossing The Threshold

Car Lafferty sat back on the porch swing. Now approaching her eighty-second birthday, and as healthy as ever, she delighted in the simple pleasures of daily life. Sunset acknowledged her, slowly moving onwards to a new place, a new land, a new way of being. An unspoken conversation bonded them.

It was her favourite time of day — watching the Sun sink carelessly over the horizon — and she gave thanks for another beautiful day. She loved sunrise, too, and truth be known, she often couldn't tell the difference such was the captivating light against the sky. The grove of Colorado spruce in the distance, stencilled against the horizon, stood like a reverent mast to the passing of another day: a day that would never come this way again.

Her thoughts were connecting dots along the story of her life: travelling to India as a young woman; her first love and only lover; the birth of her twin daughters; life on the land; and being connected to Mother Earth as she crafted her soul-led life. What a privilege it had been to watch her granddaughters and great-granddaughters and finally a great-great-granddaughter, come into this world. So much joy. So many pleasures. She wondered, for a fleeting moment, if she'd have done anything differently. Laughing, she said out loud: "Not a thing!"

Life was good. A lingering sense of contentment made her heart skip a beat as the pleasure of knowing her family were safe and all together, considering all their trials, filled her with indescribable joy. She'd spent just over forty years waiting, wondering, wishing that Astrid would be reunited with Victoria. Not a day went by where she didn't pray for her grandchild's safe return to the family fold. And for now, at least, not only had they been reunited, but it seemed as if old wounds were finally healing. It was slow, both Astrid and Mahina quite guarded, at times, even though their relationship had turned a corner, but Car trusted that they wouldn't part ways again. These past months had given Car a real skip in her step. She smiled as the Sun finally vanished from view. "Ah yes, indeed," she whispered with delight, checking no one could hear her. "It is a good day to die." It was a phrase she'd used her whole life as a way of acknowledging her blessings — one she'd learned from her mother — but since the untimely death of her granddaughter, Luna, that fateful day in the earthquake, she'd not let the words slip past her lips in case someone took offence.

So much of her life had been spent on this veranda, both with her extended family and also in solitary contentment. Here, peas were podded, cloth nappies folded, stories shared, reunions made. Even more so than the old homestead kitchen, this veranda was the heart of family life. Prayers were made, promises granted, disappointments shared. The floorboards were worn — smooth as a baby's bottom — but the heavy oak had stood the test of time. Much like Car, really.

Isaac handed Azaria a cup of cranberry tea. "So," he said, drawing her close against his body, reminding her of last night's lovemaking, forcing her to giggle as she tried to balance her cup and contain his ardour. "Can I finally pin you down and get a wedding date?"

"You really want to marry me?" she teased him, and chuckled at his persistence.

"More than anything else on this Earth. So, will you?"

"I've already said 'yes'," she laughed. "Several times, if I recall correctly," remembering that delicious day in the hot spring when he'd proposed.

"I need a date, Azaria. Pick any date you like, just don't leave it too long. Everyone in this family is relatively settled right now. No more excuses, okay?"

"Let me look at the calendar." She wriggled out of his arms and looked at the upcoming Moon phases. "Just something simple. Here, in the garden or the meadow."

"Whatever you want," he said, keen to get a date set in stone.

"Okay, how about…" she pondered, observing an upcoming Lovers' Moon. The buzzer on the oven rang out. "Hold that thought," she teased, grabbing the oven mitt Car had crocheted more than forty years ago.

Azaria opened the Aga door, smiling with anticipation and pleasure at the eggplant and potato moussaka cooked to perfection. The rich tomato and garlic sauce bubbled victoriously at the edge of the porcelain casserole dish. It was Car's favourite meal, and Azaria had made it as a treat for no other reason than to say "I love you."

The day had been long, but beautiful, as mother and daughter took a gentle stroll up through the meadows to check on the beehives, folded washing, labelled jars of honey, sewed clothes for Chandra, and chatted about how well everyone in the family was doing, all things considered.

"Life feels good, doesn't it, Mom? Finally. Like we're all moving on?" Azaria confided, knowing the grief of losing Luna would never ease, but confident that whatever Fate had in store they had the strength to face the future, even with Astrid's death always looming before them; a pewter cloud worn like a choker by the nearby horizon.

"As long as we all keep loving each other," Car said, kissing her daughter gently on the forehead, eyes misting up, "we can get through anything. You know I love you, don't you sweetheart?" Car choked up, overwhelmed by the emotion. "I'll always love you."

"There hasn't been a single moment in my whole life where I've ever been in doubt. I've always felt, somehow, that at the end of each day it's almost as if…"

"What? What is it, love?" Car asked.

"It's as if you always asked yourself 'have I loved her enough today?' You gave me enough love to satiate twenty children."

"Azaria, you know that it's because you were so easy to love. You always have been. Some people are harder to love. It's as if they wrap themselves in barbed wire, and then wonder why you pull back. Not you. Your heart was always so open. You made it easy to be a good mother. I can't imagine my life—the life I've known—had you not been there by my side. I often wonder about the sacrifice you made by living here your whole life, and what adventures would have awaited you."

"Enough! Not a single day of my life living here has been a sacrifice. Look at this place. It's a paradise. This land is beautiful. I've been blessed beyond measure to have grown up here. Why would I want to leave? Every day of my extraordinary life has been an adventure. *Every* day. I love my life, and wouldn't trade it for riches or fame. I feel like I'm the wealthiest person on the planet." Azaria hugged her mother tight. A sob caught in her chest. "You always loved me enough. Now, go and put your feet up while I make something to eat."

It would be just the three of them for dinner tonight around the old farmhouse kitchen table. Azaria looked over to Isaac who was busy setting out the plates and cutlery.

"I'll set a wedding date after dinner," she promised. "Just pop out and tell Mom that I'm serving up, will you?"

He put the linen napkins at each setting, and then kissed Azaria on the cheek before heading out of the kitchen to the veranda.

Isaac was surprised the outdoor light wasn't on, but then he knew from experience how lovely it was to watch the Sun set without the disturbance of artificial lighting. "Dinner's ready, Car," he said, stepping onto the wooden floorboards of the veranda, hearing the fourth one along doing its predictable creak. He smiled affectionately when she didn't respond. *More tired than she thought,* he said to himself. Softly, ever so softly, he rubbed her arm. "Car, it's time for dinner." She looked so peaceful, that the thought of disturbing her again seemed completely wrong. Best to let her sleep. Perhaps they should just put her dinner in the oven. He tried one more time, and that's when he noticed: there were no gentle rhythmical breaths. There was no breathing at all. "No!" he said, aware of the magnitude of the situation before him. This family — this beautiful family — was only just coming to terms with the losses of Luna, Clinton and baby Lucy, while treading carefully each day around the impending death of Astrid. Not Car. *Not now.* She was so sprightly, so healthy, so vibrant. She had more zest than most forty-year-olds. This wasn't right.

He had to tell Azaria. His heart wrenched. He thought of how happy she'd been in the kitchen, and what her plans were for the next few days. She was about to give him a date for their wedding! None of that would be happening. Everything in the family would come to a standstill. Again.

Dropping to his knees, he let the sobs fall unfettered. With his palms resting gently on Car's legs, he whispered "You were one of the most incredible people I have ever met. Thank you. Thank you for everything. Thank you for welcoming me into this family. Thank you for bringing Azaria into the world. But," the words got stuck in his throat. "Thank you for being you. Rest in peace, lovely lady. You will be missed so much."

Resting his cheek next to one of her hands, he let the tears flow. It was as if his own mother had just passed away. He stood up, slowly, forcing himself to breathe deeply. Isaac dreaded the next job he had to do, but also realised he was probably the best person for breaking Azaria's heart. This was going to crush her. Taking a long last look at Car, he admired her beauty. Her long silver hair, so regal, hung down the length of her back in well-cared-for dreadlocks. Each one was threaded with a colourful wooden or glass bead, or a miniature feather she'd collected on a walk.

The old wicker basket that had permanent residence on the veranda, filled with thick woolly blankets and throws, caught his eye. It seemed silly, somehow, but Isaac wanted to make Car comfortable. Of course, she couldn't feel the chilly breeze dancing up the mountainside or forcing its way up Isaac's spine. Wrapping her in two of the blankets she'd crocheted with her own hands, he tucked the edges in around her. "Okay," he whispered. "I'll tell Azaria now." He blew out a long, slow breath while summoning his courage and tamping the tears back inside. Isaac looked to the twilight for support.

With heavy step and tortured heart, he reluctantly returned to the kitchen. The moussaka smelled incredible.

What a waste, he thought, knowing there wouldn't be any dinner eaten tonight.

"Where's Mom?" Azaria asked. "You took your time out there."

Isaac reached for Azaria's shoulders, placing his hands over the tops of them like secure cups to hold her in place. Looking directly into her eyes, he simply said: "She's gone."

"Gone? Where did she go? She knew dinner was being made. I told her it wouldn't be long."

"Honey, she's *gone*."

"What?" Azaria asked, still not understanding the euphemism.

"My darling, your mother has passed away."

It took several seconds for his tenderly spoken words to weave their way into her heart.

The kitchen—the foundation of her whole life—swirled around her in haste. Like Dorothy in the Wizard of Oz, everything felt out of control, flying this way and that. Somewhere in the tornado she could smell the rich garlic and tomato sauce of the moussaka, and hear the sound of a Mozart string quartet on the stereo. Wildflowers on the wooden table seemed to rush by at the speed of light as she reached her arms around Isaac. The flame on the beeswax candle shivered with shock. And then, like a wild animal trapped cruelly in a steel trap, unable to break free, blood gushing from its wound, she screamed out across the night. There'd be no one else to hear her. No one, but Isaac. One day, maybe many years from now, she'd look back and realise he was all she needed.

After several minutes, Isaac whispered into her ear. "I'm going to phone Bob to help me bring Car inside. Then I'll phone the rest of the family. You should have them all around you tonight. Sweetheart, she looks so peaceful. Let everyone remember her this way. Come and sit with her."

She squeezed his hand and followed Isaac to the veranda. Only an hour or so ago Azaria was laughing in the kitchen with Car about some joke Ruby had told them. And now she was dead? How was that even possible?

Azaria looked at Isaac. "That's odd, she only ever puts a blanket across her lap, never around her. Do you think she knew?"

Isaac spoke slowly. "She didn't have a blanket on her. I…wanted to…I know it's stupid. I wanted to make her cosy." Azaria squeezed his hand tightly. That man, she loved him with all her heart. The same heart that right now was being torn in half. Again. Again!

"Thank you," her words were barely a whisper.

"Come and sit with her while I phone Bob," Isaac said firmly.

"Honey? When Bob arrives, would you place her on our bed? I think that's best. There'll be lots of room for us to take turns staying beside her."

"Anything. Anything at all."

It was about forty-five minutes later and the old Lafferty homestead was filled with the entire extended family. Azaria and Astrid lay either side of their mother, stroking her hair, kissing her cheeks, resting their faces against her bosom.

Starr picked up the guitar and strummed softly into the night, wishing with all her heart that Luna was there to sing with her. Mahina joined in, and Starr found herself smiling.

Bob brought in a tray filled with mugs of tea.

Ruby rubbed the feet of her late great-grandmother, and asked: "Now that Car has left this Earth, will someone please finally tell me why she only has four toes on her left foot? She always refused to tell me!"

Azaria and Astrid looked at each other. "I'm sure she was born like that," Astrid fibbed, wanting to protect Ruby.

"But there's a scar..." Ruby said, dragging her index finger slowly over the spot, studying it with great detail. "I'm a big girl now...come on. What's the story?"

"Another time, Rubes," Starr whispered, bringing her song to an end.

"No, I want to know now."

"Rubes!" Bella said in unison with Eliza-May.

"She dropped an axe on it," Azaria said, exasperated, the memory of that day forever etched in her ten-year-old self.

Azaria's father had tried sewing it back on because Car adamantly objected about going to hospital, but the tiny toe refused to stay attached. For weeks, it hung there precariously, the cotton thread always covered in dust and grime because Car insisted on being barefoot and carrying on as normal. One day she'd just had enough and ripped the thing off, throwing it across the garden. Azaria and Astrid refused to play outside for weeks, nightmares of it becoming a monster, haunting their every day.

"Oh, okay," Ruby said, matter of factly, absorbing the information. "So it's not hereditary or anything? My children will have ten toes?"

And with that, everyone burst out laughing. That was the thing with this family: even in the midst of grief, Ruby was there — the accidental court jester — keeping everyone entertained. Making sure their hearts stayed wide open.

The night settled in, and everyone took turns beside Car, sharing memories, expressing gratitude for her life, touching her Sun-blessed skin.

Starr found a notepad on Azaria's bedside table, and beneath the glow of beeswax candles began to write. The words came to her, flowing easy like honey on a Summer's day. Was she writing an article, or a book... maybe it was a eulogy? She had no idea.

Caroline Lafferty was more than my grandmother. She was a creative visionary, who by living a simple life brought so much joy to everyone around her. Extraordinary in so many ways, her light never failed to illuminate those around her.

I will remember her best for all the things she didn't say, even though she knew thousands of sayings and proverbs, and believe me, I've heard every single one of them dozens of times. I feel like a huge part of our family — the magnificent matriarch — has left, and yet, oddly, that space has been filled beautifully by all the women in this room. Women who walk this Earth all because of Car.

She was a grandmother in the truest sense of the word: GRAND mother. I marvel at the women around me, and the men who bless their lives.

Despite the pain I feel right now, the truth is that there isn't anywhere else in the world I'd rather be than behind these closed doors, shrouded in a love so deep, rich and genuine, and all because of a woman who made the world a better place.

Starr looked up and saw Ruby smiling. No longer was she examining Car's foot, but was studying flower petals: blue flax, yellow buttercup, and mountain aster.

"What is it, Rubes?" Starr asked softly.

Ruby looked up, her flaxen hair framing a face so youthful it belied her wisdom. "Luna says there's a message from Car."

"What does she say?" Azaria asked, reaching for Isaac's hand, and thinking it was way too soon for a message from the spirit world.

Ruby stumbled over the words. "She's happy. Her and Luna are hugging...Car says to 'let her go'. Great-granddad is with them. Oh my god, they are all so happy." Ruby looked around the room. "Why are we crying? Why are we all so sad when they're having such a good time?"

Bob embraced Astrid, the weight of her imminent death a constant knot in a tug-of-war against their daily joys.

"Because it's going to take a long time to get used to not having her around," Azaria said, wiping the tears from her cheeks.

"Isaac," Ruby said. "I don't know what this means, but Luna says Car is showing her that yellow crocheted blanket from the veranda and said to say 'thank you' to you."

Azaria's tears slipped down her high cheekbones and she nodded gently at Isaac in affirmation that his tender gesture hadn't gone unnoticed.

"Oh, there's something else," Ruby said, hesitating.

"What?" Astrid asked.

"Luna is laughing. She is telling me that Car said

'it was a good day to die!'" Ruby shook her head to the sound of her family's laughter.

There was Car, quiet and unassuming, resting peacefully in their midst, having the last word.

Ruby tucked a flower into her great-grandmother's silver hair, and kissed her goodnight one last time.

~ *The End* ~

About the Author

Veronika Robinson is an Australian writer who lives a soul-filled life in rural Cumbria, in the far north of England. Her favourite things: home, family, Monday mornings, the scent of a eucalyptus forest after a storm, kittens, lightning, ripe mango dripping down her arms, reading by a crackling woodstove, hot sunshine, a meadow of wildflowers, cosy bookshops, friendly people, lazy Sundays, cello music, the soft light of the Moon, beeswax candles and sunrise. She is a hopeless romantic, and although she's happy to buy and grow her own flowers, isn't averse to being swept off her feet by a good belly laugh and a box of dark ginger chocolate. Veronika is married to her soulmate, and together they have two adult daughters, a composer and a writer.

You can sign up to Veronika's mailing list if you wish to be kept informed of book tours and new books, and you can follow her on Facebook, Twitter, Pinterest and Instagram.
www.veronikarobinson.com
Facebook: Veronika Sophia Robinson
Twitter: @VeronikaSophia
Blog: http://veronikarobinson.com/blog/
email: veronikarobinson@hotmail.com
#creatingabeautifullife

If you enjoyed *Sisters of the Silver Moon* and *Behind Closed Doors*, look out for the final book in the trilogy: *Flowers in Her Hair*.

About the Cover Artist

Sara Simon is an artist, illustrator, writer, and mother, from Yorkshire. She works in a teeny studio in a creative little household on the edge of the Peak District, UK, with her husband and two sons, and can see the Sun rise over the hills from her drawing board.

She has illustrated several fiction and non-fiction books for Veronika Robinson.

She loves trees, long walks, wild swimming, the sky, gardening, the sea, canoeing, camping, chocolate, cats, and reading with a torch way after bedtime. She doesn't like cooking (except cake), driving, jazz, hospitals, or being cold.

Sara's artistic career has come full circle from pencil and paper, drawing everything that stayed put for longer than two minutes; through computer-based design for print and the Internet and the high-pressure world of advertising; and then back home to the easel, in colourful paint-stained trousers, dipping her paintbrush in her tea.

9 780993 158636